AF658849

India and North East India

Mind Politics and the Process of Integration 1946-1950

Sajal Nag

2022

Regency Publications

A Division of

Astral International Pvt. Ltd.

New Delhi – 110 002

© 2022 EDITORS

First Published, 1998

Reprinted, 2022

ISBN: 9788186030769

Disclaimer:

Every possible effort has been made to ensure that the information contained in this book is accurate at the time of going to press, and the publisher and author cannot accept responsibility for any errors or omissions, however caused. No responsibility for loss or damage occasioned to any person acting, or refraining from action, as a result of the material in this publication can be accepted by the editor, the publisher or the author. The Publisher is not associated with any product or vendor mentioned in the book. The contents of this work are intended to further general scientific research, understanding and discussion only. Readers should consult with a specialist where appropriate.

Every effort has been made to trace the owners of copyright material used in this book, if any. The author and the publisher will be grateful for any omission brought to their notice for acknowledgment in the future editions of the book.

All Rights reserved under International Copyright Conventions. No part of this publication may be reproduced, stored in a retrieval system, or transmitted in any form or by any means, electronic, mechanical, photocopying, recording or otherwise without the prior written consent of the publisher and the copyright owner.

Published by : **Regency Publications**
A Division of
Astral International Pvt. Ltd.
– ISO 9001:2015 Certified Company –
4736/23, Ansari Road, Darya Ganj
New Delhi-110 002
Ph. 011-43549197, 23278134
E-mail: info@astralint.com
Website: www.astralint.com

Digitally Printed at : Replika Press Pvt. Ltd.

To
Professor Om Prakash Kejariwal
and
Deblina Bannerjee-Kejariwal
whom I owe so much

PREFACE

This is a revised version of my talk delivered at the Department of Political Science, North-Eastern Hill University, Shillong which was organised by the Indian Council of Social Science Research, North-Eastern Regional Centre, Shillong as part of their Invitation Lecture Series. It forms part of my ongoing research project on the history of Insurgency in North East India.

I take this opportunity to thank Prof. M.N. Karna, Department of Sociology, NEHU who is also the Honorary Director, ICSSR, NERC and Prof. Rupa Borgohain, Department of Political Science NEHU for chairing the occasion. No thanks are however enough to express my gratitude to Dr. C. Joshua Thomas, Deputy Director, ICSSR, NERC, Shillong. But he is a friend and I do take liberties with him.

I hope the book is able to generate the debate it intends to. I tried to attempt a fresh way at looking at the history of the region using old as well as new materials. The responsibility of facts and errors of interpretation are of course mine.

SAJAL NAG

Shillong
18.2.98

CONTENTS

"The historian who looks back will no doubt consider this integration of the states into India as one of the dominant phase of India's history"

Jawaharlal Nehru
(Quoted in V.P. Menon,
Integration of Indian States,
p. 489)

"We had demolished the artificial barriers between the States inter se and the rest of India and had indeed laid the foundations of an integrated administrative and financial structure. But the real integration had to take plae in the minds of the people".

V.P. Menon
Integration of Indian States
p. 490

ABBREVIATIONS

AICC	:	All India Congress Committee
CPI	:	Communist Party of India
HMG	:	His/Her Majesty's Government
ICSSR	:	Indian Council of Social Sciences Research
INA	:	Indian National Army
INC	:	Indian National Congress
MU	:	Mizo Union
NEHU	:	North-Eastern Hill University
NEIHA	:	North-East India History Association
NERC	:	North-Eastern Regional Centre
NNC	:	Naga National Council
PWD	:	Public Works Department
UMFO	:	United Mizo Freedom Organization

INTRODUCTION

Throughout Indian history, right from the first empire built by the Mouryas down to the British empire an ostensible common pattern has been that while the rise of empires were characterised by the integration of diverse regions of the subcontinent, its decline was marked by their disintegration. In other words a centripetal pull was engineered by the rising empires while its demise unleashed a centrifugal tendency. Despite the difference in the time and the nature of empires, it is interesting to note that the imminence of British withdrawal from India led to the surfacing of various schemes which, if actualised, would reduce British India to a conglomeration of independent states. Most important among them .were the Pakistan scheme, Azad Punjab or Sikhistan scheme, Pakhtunistan scheme, Gorkhastan scheme, United Bengal scheme, Crown Colony plan and so on. Although Churchill spoke of 'Princistan' implying perhaps one independent state, in reality many of the 562 Princely States sought to withdraw from India and their autocratic rulers dreamt of returning to their medieval days. This was not just a historical situation but also the political climate — often an inspiration — against which the developments in north east India, where many states were undecisive regarding their future, have to be understood.

The eve of British withdrawal from India was characterised by two binary opposite trends: a pan Indian sentiment seeking its culmination in the form of an integrated independent India the other was a separatist tendency seeking its independent existence. Initially the Indian National Congress which was likely to assume power from the British, was not against granting the Right to Self determination and even Right to Secession to the aggrieved constituents and agreed to prepare a constitution "acceptable to all sections of the people" and a "federal one with residuary power vested in the units."[1] But alarmed by the rising number of claims it had to be emphatic that "the Congress cannot agree to any proposal to disintegrate India by giving liberty to any component state or territorial unit to secede from the Indian Union or Federation". The post-Independent Indian State wanted to inherit as much of British India as possible and was not willing to reconcile with any portions of India opting out of India even though it stated "it cannot think in terms of compelling the people in any territorial unit to remain in an Indian Union against their declared and established will."[2]

But the political environment of the subcontinent at the end of the second world war presented an altogether different situation, where it became difficult to effect this policy as popular will was often suppressed by the ambition of the rulers. In September 1945 Wavell had already promised full self government to India. With the assumption of power by the Labour Party in England, the exit of the British from India was on the cards. The announcement came in February 1947 that they would leave India by June 1948. Although such an eventuality was logical and expected, the announcement immediately fanned secessionist tendencies. A number of schemes envisaging sovereign 'Homelands' were already being circulated. Now with the imminent lapse of British paramountcy, rulers of some Princely States dreamt of reverting to their autocratic ways by retaining their sovereignty. The task of the Nationalist government which had just taken over power from the British was to curb these disintegrative potentials, merge them with subcontinental mainland and protect the original territorial limit that they inherited from the British. "Our first task was to prevent the balkanisation of the country and to stop any possible inveiglement of the States by

Pakistan, was to bring the States into some form of organic relationship with the Centre.[3] The effective completion of this arduous task was carried out under the slogan of 'Integration'. A States Department was established under the stewardship of Sardar Patel for the purpose. The "incorporation of Indian states took place in two phases: with a skillful combination of baits and threats of mass pressure."[4] Thus by the 26th January 1950, when the Constitution came into force all the States and outlying areas were integrated fully. "By Partition India had lost an area of 364,737 square miles and a population of 81½ million. By integration of the states were brought in an area of nearly 500,000 square miles with a population of 86½ millions (not including Jammu and Kashmir)."[5]

Patel, who led this process of integration was satisfied with the outcome of the endeavour. "The great ideal of geographical, political and economic unification of India: an ideal which for centuries remained a distant dream and which appeared as remote and as difficult of attainment as ever, even after the advent of Indian independence, was consummated by the policy of integration."[6]

North east India was no exception to this process of integration. Manipur, Tripura and the Khasi states were Princely States. The Naga, Mizo and Arunachal Hills (erstwhile North Eastern Frontier Agency) though not Princely States, formed Excluded Area within British India. After the lapse of Paramountcy, Manipur continued to maintain its sovereign existence until October 1949. So did Tripura. The Khasi States merged with India through the Instrument of Accession. Naga hills initially wanted to experiment life within India for a period of ten years after which it wanted to retain its option to remain independent. Arunachal Pradesh formed a Special entity within the province of Assam. The Mizos toyed with both the ideas of merging with India as well as remaining outside India. But the popular will was in favour of the former, which clinched the issue. It was a significant episode of Indian history, not told to the rest of the people of India. This work details the processes at work within the areas of Manipur, Nagaland and Mizoram which brought about the unification of these areas with the Indian Union.

Contrary to popular notion, the region of north east India did not want an outright severance from India as soon as the British decided their intention to leave India. In fact like other parts of India, north east India also experienced both centripetal and centrifugal trends. For Assam the greatest threat was the Cabinet Mission plan which sought to tag it with Bengal and Bengali dominance. The other threat for it was the growth of Muslim population in Assam and the consequent strength of the Muslim League. Manipur and Tripura were Princely States which at least for the time being would revert to their original status after the lapse of paramountcy. The conglomeration of Khasi states were virtually Princely states; they were to decide their future. That left the Nagas of Naga hills and Mizos of Lushai hills to decide for themselves. But it was not easy. The political development in these areas were not the same as the rest of India. In fact Nagas and Lushais had just been subjugated after prolonged warfare when the Indian intelligentsia was organising a national platform for the Indians. Although the Nagas had been inhabiting the Naga hills from proto historical period, the Lushais migrated to their present habitat only a couple of centuries back. These tribals had interaction with the plains people of Bengal and Assam but had not undergone the process of Sanskritisation or Hinduisation unlike Manipur or Tripura in north east India. They continued to trouble the Ahom, Tripura, Bengal and Meithei states in the precolonial period but were never completely subjugated by any of them. It was the might of a modern State and its military power (the British in India) that subordinated them completely for the first time. With the British Flag came the Bible. The proselytisation efforts of the Christian Missionaries of various denominations was nowhere more successful than in these hills of north east India. By 1947, about eighty percent of the population of Nagas and Mizos were converted to Christianity. Colonialism along with Christianity was able to completely transform these pre-historic people. Right from their dresses to their values were altered. To use the language of B. Pakem[7] and M. Horam[8] the changes which would normally have taken a couple of centuries were packed and effected within a couple of decades. The result was a socio-cultural upheaval. The people had lost their traditional mooring and identity and were using an identity which was imposed on them by people from without. From their village based, subtribe based identity they now began to identify themselves by a generic identity. The British who they fought against for almost fifty years continually and whom they ridiculed as 'half-backed' people (after their pale skin) had emerged as their father-figures. Hence the possibility of British withdrawal from their land had not only not occurred to them; that they would have to decide their own future political identity was also never anticipated by them. Therefore, the situation created a series crises for them. It is these crises and the ways the hill people dealt with them which forms the subject matter of this work. An attempt has been made to appreciate the crises and characterise because it is the resolution of these problems which shaped the course of events in the region. The crises were of identity and autonomy, unification and confrontation, fear and apprehensions, hopes and aspirations. The dilemma and confusion created by the fluidity of the juncture in the minds of the people cannot be understood if we do not delve into the minds of the people, study the structure of consciousness and analyse the socio-political crystallization of their inner conflicts.

Sources for the history of preliterate societies are scanty. Sources which would reveal the minds of people are scantier. To supplement the documentary evidence we have used oral sources and often the regressive method. The areas covered are the hills of Nagaland and Mizoram and the plains of Manipur of north east India where the problems we are concerned with, were most acute.

In north east India there has been a general complaint that the history and society of north east India was neglected by the mainstream historians, which is justified. Now that the concept of History from below is being practiced in India to discover the pressure from below in shaping the history of modern India, the non-inclusion of north east is all the more glaring. Most of north east India is not discussed in any work where the process of India's integration or even the rise of separatist demands were discussed. Not even in Sumit Sarkar's Modern India,[9] perhaps the first national history of India written from the perspective of History from below. The section dealing with States People Movement, does not include Manipur or Tripura. There is a proud depiction of pressure from the masses for integration with India but there too the hills of Mizoram was not discussed. The signing of the Instrument of Accession by the Khasi states or the events that led to the signing and fiasco of Akbar Hydari Agreement with the Nagas are nowhere mentioned. There has been thus consistent exclusion of north east India from the history of India. Such neglect prompted the historians of north east India to take up research on the area but they failed to communicate them to the rest of India. As a result north east India continue to suffer from historiographical exclusion. But unless the stories of north east are integrated with the history of the rest of the country, a true national history can never be achieved. Historiographical integration has to be a prerequisite to national integration.

NOTES

1. Resolution of the Working Committee of the Indian National Congress on United India and Self Determination, 12–18 and 21–24 September, 1945.
2. Ibid.
3. V.P. Menon, *Integration of Indian States*, Hyderabad, 1956, 1985 edn., p. 485.
4. Sumit Sarkar, *Modern India*, New Delhi, 1985, p. 451.
5. V.P. Menon, op. cit., p. 490.
6. Quoted in ibid.
7. B. Pakem, 'Separatist Movement in North East India in T.L. Bose (ed.), *Indian Federation: Problem and Issues*, Calcutta, 1987, p. 207.
8. M. Horam, *Thirty Years of Naga Insurgency*, New Delhi, 1990 pp. 4–10.
9. Sumit Sarkar, op. cit., pp. 365–70 and 450–451.

CHAPTER TWO

STRUCTURE OF CONSCIOUSNESS

By the end of the second great war it was apparent that the British withdrawal from India was imminent. With the return of the Labour Party to power in Britain it was only a matter of time. As far as India was concerned, the immediate task of the Government was to hold the elections as the last election for the centre was held in 1934 and for the Provinces in 1937. Although the term 'independence' was not mentioned, Wavell had made a promise in September 1945 to realise full self government in India.[1] But in view of the virtual revolution in India in almost every sphere against the British, which the war-devastated Britain could not fight anymore, an early withdrawal from India seemed the only way out for the British. Although the formal announcement of British departure from India by June 1948 came only on 20 February 1947, the preparation to face the British withdrawal had already begun all over the country including north east India.

All these were a sudden rush of events for the tribals of north east India. The whirlpool of developments caught them unaware. They were generally leading a complacent life and had by now settled down to the fact of colonialism which was in the guise of paternal government after prolonged years of mutual hostility. The wild tribes were rehabilitated to a peaceful settled life. Their migratory movements ceased. The periodic famines that the Mizos faced due to the bamboo flowering was now tackled by the administration. The hardships, starvation and deaths that followed the famines were minimised as the administration imported food items and distributed it to the famine affected people. Responding to the fear and apprehensions of the tribals that they were not competent yet to participate in modern politics, there were no imposition of any constitutional reforms on them by the British. Under the British they felt that they lived with their own customs and ways of life, their own kind of politics and economics. But the end of the second world war brought a wind of comet-like changes which the tribals had not anticipated. The British decision to withdraw was very sudden and abrupt for them. Suddenly there were talks of Independence, Partition, secession of Princely states, Crown Colony Plan and so on. The tribals of north east India were bewildered by the fluidity, complications and uncertainties inherent in the situation. The juncture can be described in the word of a Naga leader:

> The Nagas made a leap, as it were, from a distant past into the glare of the present century . . . found the world greatly changed. They looked around with uncertainty and pinched themselves to be assured that all that was true . . . people became suddenly restive with the existing state of affairs. There was social unrest, economic unrest, political unrest. Everywhere there were cries for better, bigger, nobler things. The era brought a new impetus to all fields of human endeavour.[2]

COLONIAL MODERNISATION OF THE TRIBALS

The British colonialism had opened up the exclusivity of the tribals and their insularity, exposed them to the so called civilised world, altered their traditional life and style. Thus within their own confines, a gradual social upheaval was taking place. The colonial administrator and Christian missionaries working in the area had come to work in a 'tribal area'. As such they had some preconceived notions based on their ideas and experiences in the tribal life of America and Africa. They had come with a 'Civilising

Mission' to spread the words of gospel to the primitive tribes and convert them to Christianity. In their operations these preconceived notions and purpose worked. They never failed to mention the tribals that they were uncivilised while the rest of the world were civilized. Their religion and life-style needed to be changed. Even though Nagas or Mizos were proud of their head-hunting and inter-tribal warfare, these were considered acts of barbarisms. They were told that they had maintained splendid isolation from the rest of the world when they had regular interaction and inter-dependence with the plains of the foothills. They were not allowed to live alone but were not permitted to move on their own. The administrators and Missionaries insisted on retaining their typical, precolonial tribal look and treated them as Museum pieces[3] when their own society had stopped the manufacture of those traditions.[4] The educated among them found it pejorative that though their tribal society had lost their pristinity and were on throes of modernisation they were constantly referred to as Tribals and Primitives, still unacceptable to the apostles of modern civilisations. The British administration through devices like Inner Line Regulations and Excluded Areas Act etc. confined the tribals to their own area when it actually was purported to keep the non-tribals outside the tribal lands. With the coming of the reforms a new culture of education and politics percolated down to these hills too which resulted in the gradual politicisation of these essentially apolitical people in the sense of modern bourgeois political practices. In the words of a Naga elder, these people were stopped in the middle of their history and a plethora of exogenous forces were let loose on them which were external to them. With the consciousness was related their identity. The tribals identified themselves with their village which was their world — their *hnam* as far as the Mizos were concerned and *lim* as far as the Nagas were concerned. But the British addressed them by the identity which the plainsman used. Thus the British gave the tribes the same name and through Census reports, official communications and tour journals popularised these names as tribe or subtribe identification which began to be gradually used by the tribals themselves. Thus the identity which the tribals used was not only imposed on them by the British the consciousness of them being different from the so-called Indians was also constructed by the same regime. For example, John H. Hutton while presenting the case to the Indian Statutory Commission had asserted that the tribals of north east India were racially, linguistically, culturally, politically and even economically different from the Indians. N.C. Parry who presented the case of Mizos put forward the same argument. Sir Robert Reid, Governor of Assam (1937–1942) stated that "they (the tribals of North East India) are not Indians in any sense of the word. Neither in origin nor in appearance, nor in habits, nor in outlook and it is by historical accident that they are tagged to Indian province (Assam)" and hence "we have no right to allow these great body of non Indian animists and Christians to be drawn into the struggle between the Hindus and Muslims which is now and will be in future with ever increasing intensity the dominating factor in India proper."[5] A.G. McGall the popular District Superintendent of Lushai Hills (Mizoram) also reiterated the proposition saying "we have come to see very clearly that the Lushai is bound rather to the Mongolian than to the Aryan races. This brings the whole question as to whether it would not be better for the Lushai to seek shelter under the colonial or Dominion offices (rather than India)."[6] Alistair Lamb wrote "the people of hills along the southern edge of Brahmaputra Valley and Burmese frontier tracts (like the Mizos, Nagas) —none of these could be described as Indians if that term was to be defined on the basis of culture."[7] On the basis of such premises some of the colonial administrators proposed the idea of a separate state under colonial control for the tribals of the region outside India or Pakistan or Burma, which were embodied in the Crown Colony Plan or the North East Frontier Province Plans. These plans eventually petered out but the ideas remained. These ideas not only formed the basis of a non-Indian identity but also influenced the idea of separate, independent states. As part of these imposed identity the tribals were told that they had maintained splendid isolation from India when in reality they had constant interaction with the Indian Plains which had been stopped somewhat only at the advent of the British. So far the distinction, if any was between the hills and plains; but from now on it was going to be between India and non-India; Indo-Aryan plainsmen of India and the hills people of north east India with Mongoloid features. Again, the assumed patronisation to the tribal cause by the British administrators embodied in the various plans were received by the gullible tribals as sympathetic and paternalistic. In fact it was also said that Adams, Advisor to the Governor of Assam on the eve of British withdrawal from India reportedly advised the Naga leaders to accept whatever terms the Indians offered to them for the time being as India was anyway going to disintegrate within next five years subsequent to which they could also have their own nation-state.[8] There were no counter to these ideas which were making rounds and were gradually turning into beliefs nor were there any counter rhetoric from the Indian nationalists to allay their fears and misgivings.[9] If at all there was any, it was a straight case of the tribals being taken for granted and their simplicity and political naivette exploited as shall be seen subsequently.[10] The hesitation of the tribals were thus converted into reluctance by the disintegrationist political environment of the nascent nation-state. The multiple number of withdrawal announcements encouraged the Nagas and the Mizos too to think in terms of separation and withdrawal. The precedents and examples were already there; the lead was there too. They just had to decide about their withdrawal. In a political climate where secessionist and separationist ideas seemed to thrive, the tribal leadership found it easier to contemplate withdrawal rather than merger. But there was also a stream of thinking which was not in favour of outright severance of ties with India, as can be seen later.

CHANGING IMAGES

The hillmen both the Nagas and the Mizos had a relationship of interdependence with the plains people of the Ahom, Cachar and Bengal states respectively. If the Nagas and

Mizos were dependent on the plains for their outlet, to barter their products, to procure items which were scarce in the hills and most important for the perpetration of raids and head-hunting, the plains of Brahmaputra, Barak and Surma Valley too were dependent on the Nagas for salt, herbs, medicinal plants, elephants tusks, rhino horns, rubbers and other such forest products. Therefore, the image the tribals built of the plains men was that of friendly folks. At the same time these plains people were also easy preys to the frequent tribal raids, kidnappings and head hunting. The plainmen were terribly frightened of these tribals who would descent from the hills without any warning or hints and perpetrate raids on them, kill their people and carry some of their heads as trophies. Often number of plainsmen were kidnapped and taken to the hills as slaves or prisoners. For the tribals, these raids were to extend the area of their territory and assert their sovereignty over these people. In fact the area where they committed these raids were considered by the tribals as their estate and the inhabitants of the region as their subjects. As such the tribals had not developed any great regard for these plainsmen and viewed them as their subjects who were weak and inferior, incapable of defending themselves. It is interesting to note that on the one hand the plainsmen considered these hillmen as savage and barbaric on account of their raids and plunders and on the other the Naga and Mizos too looked down on these plainsmen as low in terms of civilisation as they proved to be weak against the tribals invasions. They failed to protect their own standing crops from devastation by the tribal raids, protect their women and children from the tribal attacks and their technique of warfare and technology too backward to be effective to thwart the tribal attacks. It need to be mentioned that the precolonial states of Manipur, Tripura, Cachar or Bengal did not initiate any counter attack to protect their subjects on the plains bordering the Naga or Mizo hills. As such these villagers were left to defend themselves which they failed to. On tribal raids they were either helpless victims or onlookers or runaways. In fact the inhabitants of the foothills lived at the mercy of the tribals which made the

Naga and Mizos feel mighty and a symbol of terror vis a vis the plainsmen. The Memorandum submitted to the Indian Statutory Commission (1929) by the Nagas made a proud reference to this. The tribals therefore, had no occasion to view these weaklings as any kind of threat because in this tribal non-tribal relationship it was the hillsmen who were powerful and the arbiter.

By the forties of the twentieth century there was a metamorphosis of image as well as reality. A century of colonial rule had transformed this image and reality. When told that not only the British were going but it was the plainsmen who were going to replace them as the rulers, the idea was resented by the tribals. The colonial rule, detribalisation, christianisation and exclusion had changed the tribals too. They had mellowed down. Their ideas and images changed and now they had a western educated middle class leadership to lead them with ideas and actions. They had hardly any war since the last war against the British conquerors. Head hunting and raiding on the plains had been stopped. The missionaries and the British administrators made them aware that it was not the plainsmen but the tribals themselves who were backward and savage. The constant reference to them as 'tribals' and their 'primitive ways' made them conscious of this. The introduction of modern hygiene, medicines, dresses, haircuts, schools, churches and so on by the missionaries and their proven effectiveness on them were an eye-opener. With the advent of consciousness of their primitiveness came insularity. The hitherto confident tribes who considered themselves 'mighty and superior' vis a vis the plainsmen now became exclusive and lacked the confidence of dealing with them. Another cause of their inconfidence was that the missionaries and colonial administrators constantly presented the plainsmen to them as hostile people. The presentation of the plainsmen opposed to everything that the tribals were — from looks to food — had a devastating impact. The tribals could not foresee themselves as 'equals' or 'compatibles' in the prospective Indian society and polity. Their personal interaction with the plainsmen in the colonial period showed that they were treated as 'untouchables' in the hierarchical Indian social structure. They were told that now that they were Christians, they were more unacceptable in the Indian society. Their Mongoloid looks, their Tibeto-Burmese languages and their other cultural traits did not strike any similarity with the dominant Indians. In fact they realised that they had nothing common with the Indo-Aryan Indian socio cultural fabric. They stated in their Memorandum to the Simon Commission, "Our languages are quite different from those of the Indians and we have no social affinities with either the Hindus and Muslims. We are looked down upon by one for our beef and by the other for our pork and by both for our education which is not due to any fault of ours." India, thus, under changed circumstances was a world they were hardly familiar with and Indians a people they could hardly identify with. The India and Indians, they knew were only the foothills and border tracts and its inhabitants. That too had been the story of the pre-colonial times. The colonial masters had prevented them from continuing such interaction as a result of which the two communities had become alien to each other. Momentous changes had taken place since then both in the hills and plains. Even the image that the tribals had of the plainsmen had undergone change. The meek and weak plainsmen who were either subjects of the tribals or were terrorised by the raiders from the hills were now threatening to be the new masters of the hills which they strongly resented. In fact the tribals had not anticipated that a day would come when the British would leave them; worse, the white masters were going to be succeeded by these plainsmen. From the experience of colonial administration they knew that Indian rule meant the reign of the Babus — a category of people they mortally detested.[12] They did not want to be left to the mercy of these people simply because they had the experience that these people were arrogant people of the plains who looked upon the tribals as naked and primitive people; their sexual uninhibitedness and passion for carouse were frowned upon which hurt the educated tribals. This consciousness shaped the political developments of the time as far as their future was concerned.

CRISIS OF IDENTITY

Under the burden of an imposed identity and the problems associated with its perpetuation, the tribals were in a critical epistemological crisis. Their identity now was extended beyond their village and a subtribe and encompassed the generic. They were told they were hostile to Indians but now were being encouraged to join India. They were ruled as a part of British India but now were encouraged by another section to separate from India. Now they were Nagas, Mizos and so on but were they Indians or Burman ?[13] They did not know nor did anyone else had any answers for them. What they wanted was to be amongst their own people, live in their own hills to perpetuate their own customs and traditions which were so dear to them. But if the British leaves was it going to be the same ? The crisis was aptly described by a Naga leader of the time in his Memoir:

> "The political wave over India was blowing very fast and by March 1945, elders had started the Naga Tribal Association and so the questions were:
>
> a) What are the Nagas going to do ?
> b) What is the future of the Nagas ?
> c) Are we Indians ?
> d) Are we not a part of India ?
> e) What will be our future provisions ?
> f) What were are safeguards ?
> g) Where do we stand in future ?
>
> So many questions and (no answers)."[14]

The Mizos had similar dilemma. Ethnically they were closer to Burma. In fact half of the people of their tribe lived on the other side of the frontier which was now artificially created between them into India and Burma. Indeed, perhaps few other people had suffered more than these tribes who were subject to two successive partitions: one in 1937 when Burma was separated from India and another in 1947 when Eastern Bengal was separated from India. Both affected the Naga, Mizo, Arunachali, Khasi, Jaintia, Garo and Tripuri tribals severely though no one focussed on the trauma borne by these people. The Mizos except for their educated offsprings, had no concept of Indian nation. Their village, their people were their *hnam* (Mizo equivalent of nation). Those who lived close to the Burmese border felt that after the British withdrawal they would automatically be a part of Burma and would live with their brethren.[15] The Meitheis had a more serious problem. Although they were proud Hindus and were connected with India in many ways, they were being reportedly thrust into a union with Burma.[16] The Burmese Minister of Information, U.Ba. Choe claimed that Manipur had been a part of Burma which seceded from it only about a hundred years ago.[17] Now since Manipur did not want to join Muslim Bengal as envisaged in the Partition scheme, it should be back with Burma.[18] Amidst panic, another news item appeared in the national newspapers that Burmese Premier Anug San was invited to Manipur ostensibly to finalise Manipur's incorporation into Burma.[19] The resentful Meithis had a meeting on 18 May 1947, sponsored by the Manipur State Congress, to protect any such reported move.[20] Some insinuated it to be a Communist design dragging Manipuri Communist leader Irabot Singh's name into it.

The immediate reaction on the part of the tribals was to look to the British simply because there were no well meaning overtures from the Indian nationalist leadership. While on the other side of the border, the Burmese leader Aung San grasped the predicament and dilemma of the Chin tribes living on the Indo-Burmese frontier, the Assamese leaders were exactly the opposite. They knew next to nothing about the Mizos, leave alone being able to grasp the intricacies of the Mizo situation. Same was true of the central leadership of India. As far as the Meitheis were concerned, the State Congress unit of Manipur was campaigning for its incorporation into India, as will be seen later, without trying to sympathise the crisis their people were undergoing or allowing them some time. From the British too, what they received were plans to retain them under colonial rule instead of promises to grant them independence and self-rule outside India. These plans were variously named North Eastern Frontier Province Plan, Crown Colony Plan etc. There were mixed reactions to these plans:

> Most of our people were not at all aware of what was coming into the political arena of India; they just had no idea of the rapid developments that were taking place in the rest of the country. (But I had certain knowledge of what was likely to happen in India soon and which would surely affect the whole of Nagaland). I was a very hurried and worried youngman.[21]

While Rev. L. Gatpoh who represented the Jaintia hills in Assam Legislature hoped that the hills would come into the scheme of colony/protectorate,[22] his friend, colleague and minister in Assam Government, Rev. J.J.M. Nichols Roy who was returned on a Congress ticket from the Shillong Constituency took the opposite stand.[23] He informed the British Cabinet Mission that "the people of the hills who are educated and who have had experience in this political rule are greatly against such a rule." He did not think that the Protectorate idea would be economically viable. "When the whole of India will get independence", he told the Mission, "the hill people of Assam should also get their own share of independence and they should be connected with the Province of Assam."[24] Three Garos representing their people were filled with dismay to hear the rumours that there was a plan of some British officials in Assam to exclude their districts from Assam and India.[25] They opposed the plan as undesirable and demanded that their hills be joined with Assam and India. Nagas met in Kohima early in 1945 and agreed to remain in the Crown Colony provided they have their own Legislative Council.[26] Although A.Z. Phizo claimed that "the best brains of the Nagas were whole heartedly with the British in the scheme for that was a part of their spontaneous loyalty,"[27] according to a more reliable information, the Nagas "opposed it vehemently since they had no affection for any kind of British imperialism and colonialism in their land."[28] The Mizos of Lushai hills voiced their disapproval and turned down the proposal through the Mizo Union as they were hostile to the British patronisation of the Chief's rule over the Mizo people.

The other option was to look upto India which after a long struggle against colonialism was soon going to emerge as a triumphant major nation. The Cabinet Mission had suggested that there should be an Advisory Committee on the Rights of the Citizens, Minorities, Tribals and Excluded Areas. Accordingly the Constituent Assembly was going to meet and formulate such Advisory Committee where tribals representatives would be invited to participate. But it would mean joining India which had a new image now in the tribal minds. This changed image also ensued a corresponding fear and apprehension about Indian Rule over the tribals.

REFERENCES

1. Sumit Sarkar, *Modern India*, New Delhi, 1995, Rep., p. 418.
2. T. Sakhrie quoted in Verrier Elwin, *Nagaland*, Shillong, 1963. pp. 71–72.
3. Aliba Imti in his Memoir wrote, that in Naga hills there was a unwritten law of the Deputy Commissioner that "no tribal student could dress in the western way and to have his hair cut in the western mode. They were to dress in plain cloth as that was the dress of the tribal and to have their hair cut in the tribal way — round the head and anyone found not in this attire was to be fined Rs. 2/- a big sum those days": T. Aliba Imti, *Reminiscences: From Impur to Naga National Council*, Mokokchong, 1988, pp. 35–36.
4. The Meithei case was taken up for such discussion in L. Lokendrajit, "Identity and Crisis of Identity" in *North East India History Association Proceedings*, (Henceforth NEIHAP); Pashighat, 1986.
5. Robert Reid cited in D.R. Syiemlieh "The Crown Colony for North East India 1928–1947" in NEIHAP, Dibrugarh Session, 1981, pp. 172–178.
6. A.G. McCall, *Lushai Cryshallis* London, 1949, pp. 241–242.
7. A Lamb, *Asian Frontiers*, London, 1968, pp. 115–116.
8. A.Z. Phizo to C. Rajagopalachari, 22 Nov. 1948.
9. *The only exception was Nehru who wrote a letter to Secretary NNC* allaying their fears about Indian Rule.
10. The details of how the Assam Premier called the Naga, Mizo representatives to participate in the Constituent Assembly and opt for India is given in the next chapter.
11. Memorandum to the Indian Statutory Commission by the Naga Club, Simon Commission Report, Vol. XIV, London, 1930. pp. 109–110.
12. Nari Rustomji, *Imperilled Frontiers*, OUP, New Delhi, 1989m p. 29.
13. T. Aliba Imti, op. cit., p. 29.

14. Ibid.
15. Nirmal Nivedan, *Mizoram: The Dagger Brigade*, New Delhi, 1980, p. 26.
16. K.M. Singh, *Hijam Irabat Singh and Political Movements in Manipur*, Delhi, 1979, p. 203.
17. Ibid.
18. Ibid.
19. Ibid.
20. Ibid.
21. T Aliba Imti, op. cit., p. 48.
22. D.R. Syiemlieh, 'Response of the North Eastern Tribals of India towards India's Partition' in *Indo British Review: A Journal of History*, Vol. XVII, No. 1 & 2, September–December, 1989, pp. 27–35.
23. Ibid.
24. Ibid.
25. D.R. Syiemlieh, 'The Crown Colony Protectorate for North East India: the Tribal Response' in NEIHAP, Imphal, 1990, pp. 206–211.
26. Ibid.
27. A.Z. Phizo, to C. Rajagopalachari, 22 November 1948.
28. Asoso Yonou, *The Rising Nagas: A Historical Study*, Delhi, 1974 pp. 107–159.

CHAPTER THREE

PATTERN OF MOBILISATION

Although the Naga and Mizo tribes or the Meitheis were apolitical in terms of newly introduced bourgeois politics, the newly emerged middle classes were not so. They were completely equipped with the nuances of such political processes and even realised the weaknesses of their communities vis a vis participation in such politics. What was significant, they had learnt the nationalist discourse and the power it held over any other discourse. These middle classes were the pioneer of momentous changes that these areas witnessed during the next decades. The British in successive Census Reports enumerated the hill population and showed that various tribes in the Naga-hills were subtribes of one generic tribe — the Nagas or Mizos, which was a revelation to the respective tribes themselves. So far they had thought in terms of these so called subtribes only and formed political associations accordingly, e.g. Ao Students Association, Angami Students Association, Lushai Student Association, Paite Student Association and so on. Now the middle class leadership took initiative to form associations which would represent themselves as one tribe and not numerous sub-tribes. This was a result of the consciousness that in bourgeois politics numerical power of communities reflected competitive strength and vice versa. The Christian Missionaries had introduced Roman script for the yet-unwritten tribal languages. The detribalisation effort of the Missionaries had also reduced the inter-tribal feuds and head-hunting substantially and brought closer interaction between various tribes of the Naga hills and Lushai hills. The middle classes of these respective areas, now-well-versed with the nationalist discourses now found nationality or nation as more powerful concepts. The integrationists presented themselves subnationality of the prospective Indian Union while the secessionists presented the claim of separate nation-hood. Such construction was irrespective of the historical evolution of respective groups and was based purely on the power of such discourse and the ideas of the middle classes of what kind of polity they foresaw for their people vis a vis their own aspirations in that set up. Thus concepts like nation, nationality, ethnicity, sovereignty, independence, colonialism, expansionism began to be rampantly thrown. A section of the Naga, Mizo and Meithei middle classes were now ready to accept the hegemony of the middle classes of the rest of India while the other section sought to challenge it and take them head on. As far as the Indian middle classes were concerned they welcomed these weak and late-coming hill leadership under their hegemony but not the challenge. Thus a confrontation and crisis situation was inevitable in the north-eastern part of India.

Responding to their fear and apprehensions, there were no imposition of any constitutional reforms on them by the British administration. But no well meaning gestures from the Indian leadership. In fact if at all, it was from the Indian National Congress which in its Faizpur (1936) condemned the Colonial devices like Excluded Areas and Partially Excluded Areas which it felt was "another attempt to divide the people of India into different groups with unjustifiable and discriminatory treatment and to obstruct the growth of uniform democratic institutions in the country . . . the separation of these Excluded Areas and Partially Excluded Areas is intended to leave a larger control of disposition of exploitation of the mineral and forest wealth in those and keep the inhabitants of those areas apart from the rest of India for their easier exploitation and suppression. Such attitude created suspicion in the minds of the tribal middle classes.

The Political Process

One immediate response to the rush of events and the insecurity and fears it generated in the tribal minds was to politically activate themselves. It was realised that to safeguard their interests and aspirations they must come out of their insularity and participate in the political processes. Such participation in the bourgeois political process required solidarity and unification of the tribes to equip themselves to combat the hegemony and dominance of the prospective post-colonial state of India and more important, to resist being taken for granted and be allowed to decide their future themselves.

This unification and solidarity movement developed at three levels. One, at the level of all the tribes of north east, two, at the level of each subtribe and the last at the level of each generic tribe.

At the level of the tribals of north east, leaders belonging to various tribes, realised the necessity of unification of all the hill people in a single but federal unit and to articulate their political aspirations. Initially they formed the Hill Leaders Union (1945) at Shillong which worked for the welfare of the Hill areas of Assam. Prominent among its founders were Capt. Lyngdoh, Rai Bahadur Rupmei, McDonald, Rev. J.J.M. Nichols Roy and J. Marak. There was also a move to unify the hills and the plain tribals which got articulated in the formation of The Plains and Hills Tribals and Races Association (1945). But both the organisations petered out within few years.[1] Then the tribal students studying at Calcutta formed an organisation such called the 'Indo-Burma Movement' (1946) whose aim was "to unite into one unit all the party of the land lying along the border of India and Burma and other adjacent areas which are inhabited by a similar kind of people and which can be conveniently demarcated into a unit; the unit thus formed be designed as 'Indo-Burma' and the people dwelling in it be called collectively Indo-Burmans whilst retaining their tribal names separately (Indo-Burma and Indo-Burman may be changed if better names can be found). The future status of Indo-Burma thus formed (whether it will be an absolutely independent unit; an autonomous unit in free India, a part of Burma or Assam etc.) will be decided by the representative body of the peoples."[2]

At the level of subtribes there were already organisations like Ao Students Association, Angami Student Association, Paite Association etc.

At the third level there were moves to organise all the sub-tribes into one generic unit under one organisation. Here too the initiative had to come from the students who emerged as the natural leaders of their people.

> "We did not have many leaders just a handful of them and all of them were Government servants. So even before I appeared my final B.A. examination our leaders wrote to me that I should come and join the Naga People in their search for answers to so many questions . . . events took place so fast especially after Mountbatten took over as Governor General and Viceroy, that I had (to) open the Naga National Council office at Kohima on the first of November 1946."[3]

Prior to the formation of Naga National Council there was the Naga Club which was the main centre of social and political gatherings. Charles Pawsey, a civil servant working in Naga hills for years together established the Naga Hills District Tribal Council which united all the Nagas and merged all the Tribal Councils that existed among the various Naga tribes. But the fast changing political scenario in the subcontinent threw Pawsey's plan in a quandry and his incipient Tribal Council had now been turned into the Naga National Council at a meeting held by representatives of different tribes in Wokha, the centre of Lotha Nagas in February 1946. It primarily aimed at representing Naga interests and mobilising support to the British officers working for social, economic, political and cultural development of the Nagas. Originally it consisted of 29 members, representing various tribes and published a monthly newspaper entitled 'Naga Nation'. It marked a momentous event for the Naga people:

> "Our people were yearning for a change in our way of life because we were aware of the changes that were

taking place near and around us but we were still chained to the old way of life and this was the reason why the whole Naga people welcomed the starting of the Naga National Council and freely exchanged our individual views and problems. Public opinion till that period was very much restrained because of the policy adopted by the British power but when the common people saw that the Naga National Council could be their mouthpiece, the spontaneous response was most encouraging."[4]

At a time when the Cabinet Mission Plan for a federal India was being discussed and debated throughout the country, the Naga National Council held a meeting at Wokha on 19 June 1946 and passed a resolution that the NNC stands for the solidarity of the Naga Tribes including those of the unadministered areas. It strongly protested against the grouping of Assam and Bengal and urged that the Naga hills should be retained in an autonomous Assam in free India with local autonomy. It demanded that due safeguards be given to the Nagas who should have a separate electorate. Gopinath Bordoloi, the premier of Assam visited Naga hills in the same month to enlist support from the Nagas for Assam's cause. While doing so he assured sympathy to the Naga cause.[5]

In October 1946, the Nagas fearing the entry of Indian political parties, passed a resolution that no member of any political party (other than NNC) would be allowed to enter into the Naga hills without the permission of NNC, apart from what was stipulated in the Inner Line Regulations. In December 1946 the draft constitution of the NNC was prepared. The draft Constitution talked about preserving the customs and traditions of the Naga people and to work for the growth of the democratic self-government and material welfare of the people was subsequently adopted in 1947. But things were changing fast all around. There were unification moves all around responding to the demand of the changing times. The Garo's formed the Garo National Council, the diverse Lushai tribes integrated themselves into Mizo Union and the Khasis formed the Khasi State

People's Association in North east India. T. Aliba Imti, assuming the secretaryship of NNC, addressed a public meeting at Kohima on 6 December 1946, wherein he emphasised the need of the hour:

> "The NNC stands for the unification of all the Naga tribes and their freedom . . . and *cannot accept anything* dishonourable at the time of deliberations for our country. I know that the Nagas are a distinctive community with sufficient technical characteristics. Today *we are in the most critical time of our history.* Everything around us is moving and the time has come for us to move rightly'. *We cannot sit idle waiting to receive only what others assign us.* We must take initiative and make history of our own choice. Our destiny rests upon our shoulders . . . you are looking beyond the ocean for help. Cutting it short I declare to you that Great Britain will never endanger her foreign policy for the sake of you. Lastly never forget that you have been *excluded from every angle of life.* Who is responsible for it? I have but one word to say. *Our country is connected with India, connected in many ways. We should continue that connection.* I do not mind whether future India be a Congress Government or a League Government. But as a distinctive community as I stated before, we must also develop according to our genius and taste. Hence protection becomes inevitable. We shall enjoy home rule in our country, but on broader issues be connected with India. We must fight for it. We must get it. Keep on watching."[6]

The turbulent forties and uneven political developments affected Mizoram too. Apprehensive of their future and the uncertain present the intellectuals and 'elite' of the Mizos felt that the first necessary step for them to determine the course of their future was to have a political party of their own.

This party had to be born out of the Young Lushai Association (1930) which was a socio-religious organisation dominated by church leaders and prominent citizens of Aizawl. But the character of the would be party had to be political and divorced from the Christian church. It was also realised that the term 'Lushai' included only one of the Zo tribes and it was imperative that all the tribes be unified under one political organisation. To begin with, the name Young Lushai Association was replaced by Young Mizo Association using Mizo as a generic term to include all the Zo sub-tribes.

R. Vanlawma, who was the first Matriculate and General Secretary of both YLA and YMA took the initiative that his counterparts were taking in Naga hills, Khasi hills, and Garo hills. His worry was not only about the future of the Mizos after the British withdrawal but also rule of the autocratic chiefs. After consultation with Dahrawka and other prominent Mizo leaders, he drafted a constitution for a political party to meet the political needs of the people which were not taken care of by the non-political YMA.

Vanlawma's was not the only initiative at forming a political party. Saprawnrga and others wanted to hold a meeting in Lunglei for a similar discussion on a political party but permission was not granted to him. The District Superintendent, McDonald was aware of the strong following the young Saprawnga had at Lunglei and hence he did not like to take any risk by allowing the meeting in a place faraway from the headquarters. So he allowed a meeting at Aizawl. The British administration realised that the Mizos were no more isolated from Indian politics. It therefore became an urgent task to keep them away from the political activities of India.[7] In this task he took the help of the chiefs to influence and mould the political thinking of the people. During the II World War, the chiefs were made to take an oath to fight against the Japanese as their enemy.[8] The chiefs were loyal to the British administration all along since the time they accepted the British suzerainty. Since then the British had used the chiefs as a tool to remain in power. But the commoners detested being ruled by the chiefs who were patronised by the administration. The common Mizos were hostile to the 'idle' chiefs sitting at the top of the village hierarchy and using power and authority because of safeguards provided by the British. The tension between the '*lal*' (chiefs) and '*vantlang*' (commoners) was at its peak. The election of the circle representatives (16 January 1946) generated further tension. The District Superintendent called a District Conference in which 23 people were elected as representatives of the common people and 20 were chiefs. The District Conference which was represented by circle representatives of the commoners was supposed to be elected by household franchise at the rate of one vote for every 10 houses. This enraged the common people because they felt they should have more representatives in the conference as they were numerically more. The idea of such a disproportionate representation was conceived by the Superintendent himself on the plea that the commoners did not make any impact. The Superintendent himself assumed the position of President of the Conference. Sensing the conspiracy to perpetuate the dominance of the chiefs, the Mizo leaders requested the permission of the Superintendent to arrange a separate meeting of the commoners at Aizawl which the Superintendent had to grant in view of the growing discontent of the people. The meeting took place on 9th April 1946 wherein it was resolved to form a party of the commoners which was named as Mizo Common Peoples' Union with Vanlawma as the founder Chairman and General Secretary. The other officers elected to the Union were Lalbuaia and Hrangaia.

Vanlawma insisted on the substitution of the word, 'Lushai' by the generic 'Mizo' so that the party represented all the Mizo tribes, not just the Lushais, who were scattered all around the area — in Tripura, Cachar, Manipur apart from the Mizo hills. Vanlawma, whose brain child the party was said "The unity of the Mizo people must be maintained by a political organisation which promotes the strong ethnic and cultural unity which already exists among them."[9] Although the party remained largely a party of common people and hostile to the chiefs, the phrase 'common peoples' were omitted from the name of the party and changed to 'Mizo Union' to make it more inclusive to make the former village chiefs feel at ease with the new party. As mentioned, members of the Young Lushai (Mizo) Association were highly in favour of such a political party. Therefore they participated in it enthusiastically. The first conference of the party was held on April 25th and 26th to elect the executive. The new office bearers were:

President	:	Pachunga
Vice President	:	Lalhema
General Secretary	:	Vanlawma
Asst. Secretary	:	Lalbuaia
Secy. of Finance	:	Lalhmingthanga
Treasurer	:	Thanga

The meeting approved the following as the primary objectives of the party.[10]

1. To guide and lead the Mizo people and ultimately to an independent Mizoram.
2. To bridge the gap between ordinary Mizo villagers and the chiefs and their ministers.
3. To create better understanding among all the Mizos regardless of their localities.
4. To improve the Mizo standard of living as well as raise the position of women.
5. To air the voice of people at all times.
6. To popularise the Mizo language, so that the Mizo culture might be better understood and continued.
7. To establish a press in order to publish papers and other matters beneficial to all the Mizo people.

Rules for membership to the party were simple. One had to be a Mizo person, eighteen years old or more and pay initiation fees of 20 cents with quarterly dues of 4 cents every four months to retain membership.

Soon the Mizo Union became sizeable as a party. Now that a political party existed in Mizo hills, it began to attract the attention of the neighbouring districts such as the Khasi-Jaintia hills and Naga hills. Before Mizo Union, the Mizo hills were hardly heard of in the rest of India. Now the party Secretary Vanlawma was invited to the provincial capital at Shillong by Rev. J.J.M. Nichols Roy — a minister of Assam. The editor of *Shillong Times*, S.B. Choudhary took an interview of Vanlawma who talked about the feelings of the Mizos and the situation in Mizo hills.[11]

The first general assembly of the Mizo Union was held on September 24, 1946[12] wherein the following resolutions were adopted:

1. The Lushai hill District was to be included in Assam province after independence.
2. The District was not to be treated as excluded area.
3. Adequate representation was to be provided for in the Assam Legislative Assembly.
4. The District should manage its own legislature concerning its internal affairs.
5. All areas inhabited by Mizos were to be included in the district e.g. Lushai hill, Chin hills, Mizo areas of Manipur and north Cachar.

At a meeting in October 1946, at Thakthing Veng, Aizawl, elections were held for Councilor or village representatives. In the first meeting of the circle representatives it was proposed that the power of the chiefs to oust any villager from his area should be cut down by the Superintendent.[13] The chiefs were furious at the resolution and threatened that if the resolution was implemented, they would flout such an order.[14] As a consequence to this confrontation between the chiefs and the commoners, the Superintendent removed six chiefs. It however did not satisfy the commoners. It (the Mizo Union) "retaliated by launching a movement to boycott the chief altogether . . . the people were urged to defy the authority of the Government as well as of the chiefs and join together in a full-fledged civil disobedience movement."[15]

On 21 November 1946, the Mizo Union held a meeting at Lakhipur which was attended by Mizo representatives from Cachar, Mizo hills and Manipur. Bawichuaka, a Hmar from Lakhipur was elected President. The conference resolved unanimously that all Mizo areas in Cachar, Manipur and Chittagong should be amalgamated into one unit called Mizo district because the people of this region shared a common culture, language, religion, ethnic origin and geographical continuity.

As soon as the Mizo Union was well established as a party, the District Superintendent, McDonald, called a conference on 7th and 8th November of Mizo political leaders and chiefs. Since the British withdrawal from India was imminent, he wanted the conference to draft a constitution or *Vantlang Rorel Khawl* for the future administration of Mizoram and to prevent the Mizo hills from being absorbed by the Indian administration. "I am afraid" said McDonald "that Mizoram is going to vanish unless the Mizos learn the democratic system while the British are there. Therefore we British must teach the democratic system to the Mizo leaders."[16]

The proposals of the conference were set forth as follows:[17]

1) To confirm the existing established method of the Mizo chiefs' inheritance and maintain it, unless 4 out of 5 blocks (Lushai hills were divided into five blocks) agreed to change the method.
2) The highest political offices in Mizo hills must be held by Mizo chiefs (i.e. not the commoners or the MU leaders).
3) The number of representatives from the Mizo commoner's and chiefs should be equal.
4) To divide Mizoram into 15 sections and draw one representative each from both the common people and the chiefs for a total of 30. In addition two representatives are to come from Aizawl and one from Lungleh townships.

The proposals were not acceptable to the Mizo Union as it stood for abolition of Chieftainship and it was clear that McDonald wanted to hand over power to the chiefs. The MU leader Saprawnga in a letter to McDonald wrote "unless you allow us (commoners) to have twice as many representatives as the chiefs we feel inadequate to represent all the Mizos. Therefore we will not attend your meeting."[18]

The conference was to be attended by 40 representatives—20 each from the chiefs and commoners. Three hundred and fifty chiefs would form an electoral college which would elect 20 representatives for the conference. As against this each group of ten households of commoners would elect one representative which meant 25100 households would elect 20 representatives making it an unfair representation.

McDonald ignored Saprawnga's letter and instead propagated that some MU leaders were more concerned for their personal interests than for the future of Mizo hills. He felt that some leaders were taking advantage of the timidity of the Mizo commoners to speak out to voice their opinion. "Some Mizo citizens are genuinely concerned about the future welfare of the Mizo people. However they are too timid. They dare not say what they actually feel but merely do what their political leaders want them to do."[19] McDonald felt that such an important issue should not have been left to the leaders by the Mizo commoners. On this ground of unfair representation MU boycotted the conference. The prepared draft constitution was also subsequently turned down by the Governor of Assam for 'being too ambitious' (1946).[20]

In November (1946) itself McDonald called the Block Office bearers of the MU to Thakthing Zawlbuk to discuss the proposed constitution. At the meeting there[21] was severe criticism against the MU President Pachunga that he had no college education and therefore unfit for the prestigious Presidency of the MU. Saprawanga, then unexpectedly moved a no-confidence motion against the office bearers of the Union seeking their dismissal and new election. The General Secretary Vanlawma tried to explain that a Block Conference did not permit election which would have to wait till the General Assembly meeting. But it was of no avail. Amidst chaos the President Pachunga and General Secretary Vanlawma were toppled and Khawtinkhuma who had an MA degree was elected President. Lalbiakthanga who also had a college degree was elected Vice President. Vanlawma, the incumbent General Secretary and the maker of MU unsuccessfully tried to withdraw his name from contest while Vanthuama was nominated by Saprawnga for the General Secretary's position. When votes were cast, both of them had secured equal votes. The chairmen Lalhema cast his vote in favour of Vanthuama. Thus after this successful coup MU gained college educated office bearers. But the majority of uneducated Mizos looked at the educated leaders with suspicion. Moreover the crisis was not over yet. The no-confidence motion was moved in contravention to the Mizo Union constitution and therefore the ousted members refused to step down from office. This resulted in two assemblies and two sets of office bearers. Negotiations to unite the two assemblies and to elect completely new office bearers failed. McDonald intervened in the controversy at this point by confiscating files and over fifteen thousand rupees belonging to the MU. The quarrel eventually came to an end when the party was split into two and the assets were divided between the two.

Manipur

After the fiasco of the accession of Manipur to the federation proposed in the Government of India Act of 1935,[22] Manipur was reeling under one crisis after another which were local in character but reflected the essential tensions of a transforming structure under the influence of global changes.

In fact the phase of 1900 to 1950s has been aptly described as a 'period of social movements' in Manipur. The long popular protest movement against the prevailing system of slavery (*Minai Channaba* and *Minai Asanba*) and *lallup* (compulsory service to the state) eventually resulted in the abolition of both (1892). This was followed by a reactionary movement from the princes, who were the beneficiaries of both these forms of slavery against the abolition. Then there was the Bazar Boycott Agitation (1920), Anti-*Pathang* Agitation (1909–11), incendiarism and popular protest (1904) etc.[23] The Kuki rebellion burst out during 1917–20 against the British raj which was ruthlessly suppressed by the raj. But it was revived by Jadonang followed by Gaidinliu in (1930–1949).

The educated middle class of Manipur had started to assert themselves and react against the various oppressive socio-religious policies of the king and the Brahmins. In very broad terms there were two main trends of such reactions. The first trend, usually known as the Sanamahi Movement had semi-revivalistic character and was led by

Naorem Phullo from Cachar. Naorem Phullo Singh a Meithei, faced the hardship of a minority community in Cachar. The gripping economic problems of the Meithei peasantry, alongwith the religious as well as the cultural arrogance of the Bengali high caste Hindus in Cachar made the life of the Meitheis difficult. Phullo[24] who was working as an assistant sub-inspector in the Railway Police, resigned from his job and threw himself to the task of investigating into the causes responsible for the pathetic conditions of the Meithei peasantry in Cachar. In the process Phullo launched a programme of socio-economic regeneration of the Meitheis and founded the 'Apokpa Marup' in Cachar (1930). The Marup tried to revive the traditional religion of the Meitheis known as 'Sanamahi' and the traditional Gods like Pakhangba, Sanamahi Leimaren and emphasised the relevance of the traditional Meithei religion for the moral, social and economic regeneration of the Meitheis. This movement also devoted itself to rediscover the ancient Meithei manuscripts called *Puya*, popularise the Meithei script and desanskritise the history of Manipur. Its protagonists discarded the theory of Mahabharata connection of the Meitheis as a myth and exploded the myth of Aryan origin of the Meitheis. In his writings captioned "Meitheigi shel Chatnaba Hambi" (the causes of Meithei poverty) Phullo strongly argued that Hinduism followed by the Meitheis involved numerous ceremonies, rites and rituals which drained the resources of the people. He also exposed the exploitative character of Brahmanism and the Brahmanic clergy of Manipur. Although the Sanamahi movement could not become substantially influential then, the aspect of *Apokpa Marup* appealed to the problem-ridden people of Manipur. The educated Meithei middle class took up a different course of action. On the one hand they wanted to reform the society and on the other, they wanted preservation of Hinduism and its affiliated streams of culture. They were more interested in removing the ills of Hinduism that had crept into it over the years in Manipur rather than removing Hinduism itself.[25] Pandit Atombapu Singh (1889–1963),[26] one of the pioneers of this school of thought took up the task of translating the original Hindu texts like Bhagavat Gita, Rigveda, Geet Govinda and other such classical texts of Gaudiya Vaishnavism. The purpose of such a move was to instil a new spirit in the dying Hinduism of Manipur. In an article 'Matam Asida Maipurgi Wakhal' (social thinking on present Manipur),[27] the author Gokul Chandra Singh led a scathing attack on the Meithei Brahmins who were described as a degenerated lot who were not heeding to the call of changing times. The same line of argument was put forward in a write up in *Yakairol* which pointed out that while the general Meitheis were struggling for higher education, the Brahmins did not bother to study beyond their scriptures.[28] In a hand written pamphlet "*Houjikki Amang Aseng Amasung Madudagi Kannanaba Upai*" (The problem of Amang Aseng and the way to solve it) Irabat Singh argued that the legitimacy given by the religious authority to the civil system of Mangba-Sengba was due to the incorrect understanding of Hinduism.[29] Such evils could be rooted out by reforming Hinduism. At the same time this new middle class had progressive ideas and actions regarding encouragement to female education and advancement of overall education for Meithei youths.[30] This group of people had not only seen the contradictions of colonial rule but also the evils of monarchy itself. It was this group of emerging middle class who advocated the establishment of responsible government.

The demand for the establishment of a responsible government in Manipur is closely related with the birth of the Nikhil Hindu Manipuri Mahasabha, a socio-religious organisation which was established under the patronage of the Maharaja of Manipur in 1934. The Mahasabha had all the leading personalities of Manipur in its membership list. The influence of the political development in the Indian mainland and the Indian nationalist movement activated these elite to seek a change in the nature of the colonial rule as well as the monarchical autocracy. With this aim in view the Nikhil Hindu Manipuri Mahasabha was converted into a political organisation called Nikhil Manipuri Mahasabha. It came about in the fourth session of the erstwhile socio-religious organisation held at Imphal on 30th December 1938.

The composition and the political affiliation of the members of the Mahasabha clearly revealed that the Mahasabha was constituted by two groups of people having two different set of political objectives. One group was in favour of integration with India after British withdrawal while the other was against it. These differences were manifestly demonstrated in their later day political actions. But these differences did not create any major hurdle in the functioning of the organisation because of their identical attitude of hostility to colonial rule and monarchical autocracy.

On the eve of the outbreak of the second world war another crisis hit Manipur. To meet wartime food needs, the Government was purchasing large quantities of rice. Taking advantage of the situation the unscrupulous Marwari traders who had by this time established a firm grip over the Manipuri economy, began to buy up all the rice produced in Manipur and instead of selling them in the local market, exported the rice making huge profits. As a cumulative result the subsistence economy of Manipur faced huge food crisis. There was no rice available creating an artificial famine-like situation. Tension was high specially because the unscrupulous traders were Marwaris from Indian plains (Mayangs). The Manipuri women launched a massive agitation against the export of rice and demanded governmental interference. This movement known as Nupilan (1939-40) immediately spread like wild-fire and though led by womenfolk, drew support from all sections of the society.

The Nikhil Manipuri Mahasabha split into two over the question of support to Nupilan as one section led by Irabat Singh wanted to whole-heartedly support it, the other opposed such support. As a result of the split the faction led by Irabat Singh formed a new party called Praja Sammelani whose avowed objectives were the abolition of colonial as well as feudal rule and the establishment of a responsible government.

In the meantime, the second great war hit the world and along with it came the Indian National Army (INA) offensive in Manipur.[31] The campaign was ill timed as it coincided with the weakening of the Axis Power.[32] Moreover the INA contrary to their expectation failed to enlist the support of the nationalist leaders in India. They also failed to gain sympathy from the people of Manipur and Nagaland.[33] It would appear that Manipuris seemed to have no connection with the INA leader till 7 March 1944, when Bose's handbill containing documents and Gandhi's photo was distributed to them.[34] Even after this only a small number of Manipuris joined the INA.[35] On the other hand, the British were able to obtain supply and manual help from the Nagas and Manipuris when the Imphal-Kohima road was blocked.[36] Hijam Irabot was the only known leader to have supported Bose, but he was arrested under Defence of India Rules in 1944 and put in the Silchar jail for eight months.[37]

The post war period saw Irabat as a confirmed Revolutionary with a leftist ideology. His stint at Sylhet jail following his involvement in Nupilan had proved a training ground for him in Marxian ideology.[38] The failure of the INA was also a disappointment. He along with his Manipur Krishak Sabha intensified its socio-political reform movements. Irabot's slogan, "land to the tiller" caught the fancy of the peasants. The demand for "full responsible government", through "adult franchise" were again adopted and passed at the second conference of Manipur Krishak Sabha held at Nambol on 16 May 1946.[39] In response to the Cabinet Mission proposals, the Manipur State Praja Sammelan also reiterated the "necessity of existence of a legislature in Manipur". In its resolution, it said:[40]

> "that the Cabinet Mission and the Chambers of Princes have made a public proclamation as regards the introduction of the Legislative Assembly into those native states where the legislature has not yet been formed. The necessity of the existence of a legislature is a keenly long felt want and people have so long been enthusiastically demanding it. It takes air that the said assembly be soon introduced into Manipur. If it is a fact the Sammelan hopes that your highness the Maharaja of Manipur would graciously fulfil the long cherished hope of the Praja with a royal proclamation."

On 16 May 1946, the Manipur Krishi Sammelan was also converted into a political party. This was followed by the establishment of Manipur State Congress Party on 4 October 1946. Subsequently it became a unit of the Indian National Congress. All members of the Nikhil Manipuri Mahasabha also became members of the Congress. Like other parties the Congress also demanded the establishment of a responsible government on the basis of the principle of democracy, adult franchise and the abolition of monarchical rule etc.[41]

The imminence of British withdrawal made the people as well as the Maharaja restive. While the movement for responsible government was intensified, the autocratic Monarch dreamt of reverting to sovereignty and autocracy but sensing the peoples' mood for responsible government which he was willing to concede at this crucial juncture, he asked the British Residency at Manipur to allow him to make a royal proclamation regarding a new administration. The British political agent, Mr. Gimson asked the Maharaja to supply him a copy of the draft.[42] In course of his letter dated 30th October 1946, Maharaja Budhachandra expressed a desire to establish a democratic system of administration with an elected Advisory Assembly constituted by the representatives of both hills and plains. But in actual practice the Maharaja had prepared only a new set of Administrative Rules. Agitated, the state Congress party submitted a Memorandum on 1 November 1946 for the establishment of a proper Legislative Assembly.[43] The Maharaja sensed the belligerent mood of the people in the changed circumstances and issued a formal order (12 December) to constitute a constitution making committee to prepare a new constitution for the state. On 27 July 1947, the Committee submitted its constitution to the Maharaja. However the Maharaja was not fully prepared to implement the demand of the political parties.[44] Instead he formed an interim Government in Manipur on 1st July 1947. The Manipur State Durbar was abolished and renamed as Manipur State Council.[45] On 15 July 1947, Pearson, the President of Manipur State Durbar became the Chief Minister of Manipur. But soon he was replaced by Priyobrota

Singh, the younger brother of the Maharaja.[46] Amidst such developments, the British withdrew and on 15th August when India was declared independent, Manipur reverted back to its old status — an independent sovereign monarchy.

Rise of Separatism

The Naga move bore fruits immediately. Nehru wrote to T. Sakhrie, Secretary of the newly formed Naga National Council on 1 August 1946 assuring him of safeguarding the Naga interests and political aspirations.[47]

> It is obvious that the Naga territory in eastern Assam is much too small to stand by itself, politically or economically. It lies between two huge countries, India and China, and part of it consists of rather backward people who require considerable help. When India is independent, as it is bound to be soon, it will not be possible for the British government to hold on the Naga territory or any part of it. They would be isolated there between India and China. Inevitably, therefore, this Naga territory must form part of India and of Assam with which it has developed much close associations. At the same time it is our policy that Tribal areas should have as much freedom and autonomy as possible so that they can live their own lives, according to their own customs and desires. Thus the solution would be that the Naga territory should be an internal part of Assam province and yet should have a certain measure of autonomy for its own purposes. How this should be worked out is a matter of further consideration between the peoples concerned. So far as I can see, there is no reason why there should be any excluded area apart from the rest. The whole Naga territory should go together and should be controlled in a large measure by an elected Naga National Council. At the same time the Nagas should have representatives in the Assam provincial assembly and should participate fully in the life of the province.

I am glad that the Naga National Council stands for the solidarity of all the Naga tribes including those who live in the so called unadministered territory. I agree entirely with your decision that the Naga hills should constitutionally be included in an autonomous Assam in a free India with local autonomy and due safeguards for the interests of the Nagas.

As for separate electorates for the Nagas, I am not clear in my mind as to how this will work. Generally speaking, we are against separate electorates as these limit and injure the small group by keeping it separated from the rest of the nation. But if the Naga territory is given a measure of autonomy, some arrangement will have to be made for their proper representation.

As you know the Congress is opposed to any forcible grouping of Assam with Bengal. We are of the opinion that this is a matter for each province to decide. Assam has already expressed its opinion on the subject. What the future will be, I cannot say, but I cannot conceive of Assam being compelled against its will to form a group with Bengal.

An Advisory Committee will be elected by the Constituent Assembly. It should have representatives of the Tribal areas and I hope the Tribal territories of Assam will be directly represented on it. The findings and decisions of the Advisory Committee will probably not be finally binding upon the Constituent Assembly but they are bound to carry great weight. I imagine the findings will be accepted almost in their entirety unless they go against some direct provision in the Constitution.

As I have said above the Excluded areas should be incorporated with other areas. It may be that certain special provisions for their protection and development will be made. I should like them to be treated as part of the entire Naga territory.

I see no reason whatever why an extraneous judicial system should be enforced upon the Naga hills. They should have perfect freedom to continue their village panchayats, tribal courts, etc., according to their own wishes. Indeed it is our wish that the judicial system of India should be revised, giving a great deal of power to village panchayats.

About the unadministered territory which still contains, according to you, a number of head-hunters, I cannot definitely say how soon and in what manner it should be brought into the province. This is to be devised in consultation with the people concerned. Naturally some special provisions will have to be made to develop these people.

The question of common language must also be finally decided by the Naga themselves. The only two possible languages which would be helpful to them are Assamese or Hindustani. Most of them know some Assamese already. I think it would be desirable to encourage Hindustani as this will bring them in touch with the various changes and developments taking place in India.

Assam is still largely undeveloped and there is plenty of room for agricultural, horticultural and industrial development. This development should be so organised as to benefit the people of the soil. Certainly the people of the Naga hills should not be exploited by others, and their right to own and work on the soil should remain with them. We should be entirely against the development of large estates owned by outsiders there. What form land ownership should take, whether it should be communal, co-operative or kind of peasant proprietorship, should be determined in consultation with the people concerned.

I might add that I am specially interested in these Tribal areas not only in the north-east of India but in the north-west as well as the Centre. They present different problems. I hope that in an independent India there will be special department, both in the Centre and in the provinces concerned, for the protection and advancement of Tribal areas. I do not want them to be swamped by people from other parts of the country who might go there to exploit them to their own advantage.

Gopinath Bardoloi, Chairman of the Committee of the North East Frontier Tribal and Excluded Areas Committee as a part of the Cabinet Mission proposals visited Aizawl in April 1947. McDonald, the District Superintendent presented the District Conference's demands to Bordoloi.[48] The demand included (1) representation of at least three seats in the Assam Legislative Assembly; (2) administration of land tenure, agriculture, social customs, primary education, immigration, civil and criminal justice by the District Conference of Lushai Hills District; and (3) self-government by the Zo people in accordance with the Constitution approved by the Indian Government. The Government would also be required to pay a certain amount as grant-in-aid.

On 17th and 18th April, 1947, the members of the Advisory Sub-Committee of the Constituent Assembly visited Aizawl. The Mizo Union, submitted a memorandum which contained the following points:[49]

> . . . At the time when India becomes Independent, the present Lushai hills District also will be federated with the Province of Assam and be connected therewith in certain subjects which shall be desired by negotiations between the provincial legislature and the Mizo National Council. The District will henceforth be called 'Mizoram' including contiguous areas of Cachar, Chittagong hill Tracts, Manipur and Tripura. 'The village with its village council will constitute the unit and basis of administration with Mizoram. . . . There shall be a Legislative Council . . . and Executive Council."

It went to state that out of 27 members in the Legislative Council only 'two members for the village chiefs or headmen should be elected by the chiefs or headmen themselves according to the rules prescribed. . . . No non-Mizo will be qualified to stand as candidate.' The draft constitution prepared by the Mizo Union contained the following paragraph 'In a backward *nation* (emphasis mine) like the Mizo it is desirable that a complete separation of powers between the Legislative, the Executive and the Judiciary as possible be maintained . . . there shall be *no capital punishment in the country*. It stated that the special Financial Provision to Mizoram should be made by 'the Centre from year to year until such time as the Mizos shall assert that they are able to maintain their territorial integrity and self determination without this financial provision.' It lastly stated that 'all the points suggested by the party shall be subjected to revision after ten years.

Prior to this, Bordoloi telegraphed Vanlawma to come to Shillong, capital of Assam to attend a meeting of all the representatives of Assam, of which Lushai hills was a district to determine whether the State in general wished to join India or Pakistan (in view of the Cabinet Mission Plan proposals). Bordoloi needed to mobilise opinion and votes to resist the proposal to incorporate Assam in Bengal. Vanlawma was asked to opt for India.[50]

Vanlawma was in a very difficult situation:

> "It was very difficult to make a decision by myself without consulting my colleagues as we had not made any decisions beforehand. Most of us wanted to become independent, but some chiefs refused to follow any decisions taken by the Mizo Union. So it was next to impossible to take steps for independence, but we were not in a position to opt for India. But decisions had to be made. If we refused to help India and failed to fight for independence, India or Pakistan might impose status which we might not be able to object to. So I was of the opinion that it would be better to bargain for the best status that India could offer."[51]

To strike a bargain Vanlawma expressed his apprehension, fears and misgivings and asked for safeguards.

> Look here Mr. Bordoloi. See the town of Shillong which is the capital of the Khasis. You would not find a single Khasi merchant in the business area. Do you think I

will make Aizawl like Shillong? We are most afraid of economic exploitation by the business experts from the plains. The papers in Shillong and Calcutta are demanding the 'Black Regulations must go' in their headlines. They wanted (sic) to abolish the Chin hill Regulations and the Inner Line Regulations which are protecting us from the exploitation of the plains people. If you want our aid, my condition is to keep these regulations. . .

We are a Mongoloid stock people and coming from the east we are ethnologically and culturally different from you who came from the West. We are now Christians but even before we converted to Christianity our own religion differed quite substantially from yours and it will not be possible to live with Indians under the same laws and regulations. You are requesting me to opt for India and as a matter of fact we have the right to opt for Pakistan as well as for independence. At the same time we are financially weak and lag behind in civilization. We are a small nation and we need a great nation to depend upon. If we are going to help you, will you as an Indian leader, come forward to help us in obtaining our own legislature and administration? Will you leave us alone to manage our affairs so that we can survive among other nations."[52]

Bordoloi reportedly agreed to retain the protective Regulations and assured Vanlawma of adequate representation in the Assam legislature as well as in the Indian Parliament.[53] But Vanlawma insisted on autonomy because the Lushais might be given only two or three seats in the legislature of hundreds.

I know in the legislature matters are decided by the majority. How can a microscopic minority be heard? In the Indian parliament we would not have representation unless special arrangement are made for us. Thus there is no safeguard for us in the legislature or parliament. The only safeguard for us is separate administration or autonomy. If you 'insist on having the same

> law and regulations for the Lushai hills District, our discussion should end here. If you want us to help you keep this area from becoming a part of the proposed Pakistan, it will be your turn to safeguard our existence.[54]

Bordoloi reportedly promised to try and give the Mizos substantial autonomy, "If Nehru introduced such an autonomy Bill it would likely to be passed because Lord Mountbatten was a friend of Nehru's and would support the proposal." Bordoloi also reportedly, assured Vanlawma that no law which might jeopardise the survival of the Mizos would be forced upon the Lushai hills district. The two men also agreed, reportedly that matters of finance, defence and communication should be under the control of the Central Government.

> Vanlawma and Bordoloi concluded their talks with a *gentleman's agreement*, whereby Vanlawma as representative of the Mizo Union would opt to join India, and Bordoloi, as the Chief Minister of Assam would obtain autonomous status for the Lushai hills District.[55]

Bordoloi also asked Vanlawma to accept membership in the sub-Advisory committee on Tribal affairs which was to be formed by the Constituent Assembly to which Vanlawma agreed.[56]

On his return Vanlawma found T. Sakhrie and Phizo, the Naga National Council leaders in Aizawl to enlist the support of the Mizos in their struggle for 'independence'.[57] They asked Vanlawma to declare independence of Lushai hills and even offered to merge Lushai hills and Naga hills to form one independent country whose official language could be the Mizo language.[58] Vanlawma in view of his commitment to Bordoloi promptly turned down the offer.[59] But when the Sub-Advisory Committee of the Constituent Assembly on Tribal Affairs under the Chairmanship of Bordoloi was formed, Vanlawma had already been toppled from his Secretaryship of the MU. The new President of the party Khawtinkhuma and Saprawnga were offered co-opted membership in the Sub-Advisory Committee.

Vanlawma asked the two members not to accept co-opted membership and demand full-fledged membership because the Committee had Naga, Khasi and Jaintias' as full-fledged membership.[60] It was also considered a violation of the 'Gentleman's Agreement' that Vanlawma had with Bordoloi.[61] In such a situation the two MU office bearers' acceptance of co-opted membership was viewed as 'unnationalistic' and 'yielding to the wishes of the Indians'.[62] District Superintendent McDonald was also alarmed by the situation and attempted unsuccessfully to block the membership of Khawtinkhuma.[63]

The two members' return from Guwahati in early 1947 after confirmation of their co-opted membership raised a hue-and-cry from the opposition. In a public meeting held in Aizawl to review the situation Vanlawma expressed his bitterness over the violation of his agreement with Bordoloi and demanded that, on this ground of untrustworthiness, the Mizos should refuse to be in India and declare complete independence.

> In the ancient past Mizoram was not under anybody's governance. Now that the British who controlled us are about to leave the Asian subcontinent we should resume the status we held before the arrival of the British. We should demand total independence. . . .[64]

The Mizo attending the meeting were greatly agitated. Some were for independence and others were fearful of the consequences of independence. There was a public debate on the issue. Replying to the question as to why the MU had not aimed at independence right from its inception but was being raised now, Vanlawma said:[65]

> When we formed Mizo Union party the British administration was not clear as to when and how they were going to leave India. Under them the country was taken care of nicely and if we had mentioned independence when we started Mizo Union party, the British would not have let us start it at all. But now that India is going to obtain independence, we feel that they will be ruling our country and not considering our own interests. However the attitude of the Indian people is

> becoming clearer. They failed to carry out their promise to us: that we would have full membership on the planning board and have asked us to be co-opted members only and might intend to give us still less than self-determination in the future. Now that we know that they are not going to carry out their promises our future looks very uncertain. Therefore we must govern ourselves. At the moment we have enough supplies and if we lack supplies we will still find some other country to help us. And if we look at our natural resources and increase our produce by improving our farming system we will be able to produce a sufficiency of things. Now is the time to fight for our independence.

The defendant, Vanthuama, General Secretary of MU stood up and replied:

> It is impossible for us to fight for our independence now. If we look around us, we see the Darwin theory — the more powerful swallowing up the less powerful. If and when we are truly more powerful, we will swallow the Indians and if they are more powerful than us, then they will swallow us. Besides if we are independent where will we get salt and iron ore to make our farming equipment and how are we going to make money.[66]

There was sharp differences between the two sections of the public. The meeting took the form of debate between Vanlawma and Vanthuama representing two schools of thought. Vanlawma replied to Vanthuama's argument saying:[67]

> Pu (Mr.) Vanlawma's statement on Darwin's theory seems to me to be an attempt to escape reality. We all know for sure that we, the Mizos are much smaller and less powerful than the Indians. For that very reason we created the Mizo Union Party. . . .

> Concerning salt and iron ore our ancestors, though less advanced than we, were self-sufficient and even made their own guns. If our ancestors knew how to trade with their neighbours we certainly ought to be able to

take care of our own affairs. Concerning money we can use it as the rest of the world does. If we have enough food there is no need infact to be unduly alarmed about our future.

Thus the meeting even divided the residents of the Aizawl town into two. The southern localities of Aizawl were in agreement with Pu Vanthuama against independence and the northern localities of Aizawl were in agreement with Vanlawma, supporting independence.[68] This meeting marked the emergence of a new concept, that of total independence.

By the beginning of 1947 circumstances in the Indian subcontinent were changing very fast. The imminent independence of India, its partition, withdrawal attempts by princely states, creation of an Independent United Bengal and Sikh homeland were the news and discussions that filled the air. There were decolonisation process, withdrawal of the colonial powers and freedom of the colonised countries taking place world over. "Nagas too fell in the same curious chain of processes."[69] The Nagas were sure that they needed self-rule to safeguard themselves. They were encouraged by the Muslim League victory and the colonial schemes to create a separate area for the tribals. Against this background the political stand of the NNC also underwent a change which now desired securing a predominant political position for the Nagas. Soon they started thinking in terms of complete independence from India rather than an autonomous unit within the Assam province.[70] "At last they, filled with patriotic enthusiasm, voiced out from a moderate demand for regional autonomy in Assam to outright sovereign independent Nagaland without giving due consideration to the concept of Crown colony or a Trust territory under the UN charter as they were apprehensive of losing their identity with the disappearance of British rule in the midst of Hindu rule."[71] But they also tried to balance this demand by accommodating the idea of a section of the leadership that it was not advisable to outrightly severe all ties with India. Hence a ten year interim period within India was inserted. A resolution was adopted to this effect by the NNC on 20 February 1947 and submitted to

His Majesty's Government and the Government of India. The Memorandum stated:[72]

> The Naga people were independent and their country was not subjugated by the Ahom Kings of the Assam Valley, who ruled over for seven hundred years. They never formed part of Assam or India at any time before the advent of the British. Little was known of Nagaland when the British obtained suzerainty over the Assam valley by the treaty of Yandaboo. The British first attacked the Naga people in 1829, but the fight went on for fifty years till the Ao country was taken over in 1869. Since then the Naga people have remained loyal, friendly and peaceful. In the first World War thousands served in distant France to help the British and the allied cause. In the recent second World War, when the Japanese army attempted to invade India through Nagaland, it was the co-operation of the Nagas both in intelligence and jungle warfare which enabled the British forces to halt the invasion at Kohima, the headquarters of the district, thus saving Assam and the rest of India from the devastations of war.
>
> These freedom-loving Nagas look up to HMG and the Government of India to do the just and proper thing and grant them their just demand for setting up an interim Government of Naga People. As the Modern World recognises the importance of psychological implications dealing with nations to have peace within the without, it is necessary to know the tradition and national aspirations of people and to respect them. The attitude of a people has a great bearing in the formation of national policy.
>
> In framing the constitution of India certain thought provoking factors must not be ignored:
>
> i) Ethnically Nagas are from a distinct stock.
>
> ii) They have a distinct social life, manner of living, laws and custom and even their method of governance of the people is quite different.

iii) In religion, the great majority of the Nagas are animists but christianity which was introduced by the American Baptists long before the advent of the British rule is now speedily spreading. Such factors as the above make it imperative that the Nagas should have a separate form of Government. The Nagas have an efficient system of administration. Most of the tribes retain to a considerable degree their ancient laws and customs and village organisation which have lasted through centuries, and these form an integral part of their life and once destroyed or allowed to decay, can never be replaced by a system so suitable to them. Democracy in its purest form exists among the Nagas. The basis of the Naga system is the village organisation. Every village is a sovereign independent unit in the tribes. Village is managed by a council of elders and men of influence elected by the people. Such a polity, such a state of society and democratic life cannot be found in any other part of India.

In the 1935 constitution for India and Assam, the areas inhabited by the Nagas were kept outside the jurisdiction of the provincial and central popular governments and were formed into 'Excluded Areas', where the legislatures had no way and the Nagas were kept under the special responsibility of the Governor of the Province in his capacity as the Crown Representative. In other words, the Naga people have had no connection with the policies and politics of different groups of Indian politicians. Ought the British Government or the Government of India throw this society into heterogeneous mixture of other Indian races? A constitution drawn by the people who had no knowledge of Nagaland and the Naga people will be quite unsuitable and unacceptable to the Naga people. Thrown among forty crores of Indians the one million Nagas with their unique system of life, will be wiped out of existence. Hence this earliest plea of the Nagas for a separate

> form of interim Government to enable them to grow to a fuller stature should be acceded.
>
> In the light of the facts stated in the foregoing paragraph and in view of the isolated geographical position of Nagaland and taking consideration of the Naga polity and the compact block of Nagaland, this Memorandum is placed with the authorities for setting up of an interim Government of the people with financial provisions for a period of ten years, at the end of which the Naga people will be left to choose any form of Government under which they choose to live.

This Resolution adopted by NNC, subsequently submitted to His Majesty's Government and the Government of India as a Memorandum, was a momentous event in the history of the Naga people for, this was the first time they demanded complete independence and severance of all ties from India which was to dominate the political life of the Nagas in future. Ten years interim government was only to enable themselves to be trained in modern political functioning and achieve economic viability. This period also could prove to be the acid test for the Nagas. If failed they could always opt for India at the end of ten years. But the changing course of events proved that it was not to be.

It is interesting to note that just before this resolution was adopted, Sir Andrew Clow, Governor of Assam, who visited Mokokchong in January, 1947, and where he met the leaders of all the northern Naga tribes, had correctly sensed the new mood of the Nagas. He, therefore, made it a point to explain to them that:

> The British Raj was being withdrawn shortly and the future Government of India including Assam and its hills will be a matter for the people of the land to decide. The Constituent Assembly, which is charged with working out the plans for the future has already started work in Delhi and it will have to consider, in due course the position of the hill peoples. They should, therefore, themselves be thinking over the question and form their own conclusions regarding what they want. It is not

practicable for the Naga tribes or even the Nagas as a whole to set themselves in a separate state or states (as some of them want) or even as a (separate) province of India. If they did they would always remain poor and backward and could not supply even the inadequate services they already enjoy. They would therefore be well advised to seek to form part of the province, but to retain matters of local concern in their own hands.

Even in the plains many matters of local concern are run by the people of the district concerned, and it here, where their customs and culture differ so much from those of the plains, they could reasonably claim a larger sphere for local authority, including control of their own land and conservation of such authority such as is traditionally theirs.[73]

NOTES AND REFERENCES

1. Information regarding the formations of both these organisations were provided by T. Aliba Imti, *Reminiscence: Impur to Naga National Council*, Mokokchong, 1988, pp. 11–12.
2. Resolution of 'Indo-Burma Movement' at December 1946, cited in Asoso Yonuo, *The Rising Nagas: A Historical and Political Study*, Delhi, 1974, p. 165.
3. T. Aliba Imti, op. cit, p. 28. This was the Kohima office. The Naga National Council had already been established in February 1946, at Wokha.
4. Ibid., p. VI.
5. The draft Constitution is available in ibid., pp. 163–164.
6. Ibid., pp. 164–65. Also see T. Aliba Imti, op. cit.
7. B.B. Goswami, *The Mizo Unrest: A Study of Politicisation of Culture*, Jaipur, 1979, p. 130.
8. Ibid.
9. R. Vanlawma, *Kan Ram Leh Kei*, (in Mizo), Aizawl, 1972, p. 90. Ramchuani Sena Samuelson's translation adopted here as well as in subsequent note.
10. R. Vanlawma, *The Mizo Union*, Aizawl, 1946, pp. 1–2. Cited in Ramchuani, Sena Samuelson, *Love Mizoram*, Imphal, 1985, p. 30.
11. Vanlawma, *Kan Ram etc.*, op. cit, p. 97, cited in ibid, p. 31.
12. Ibid., p. 107.
13. Vumson, *Zo History*, Aizawl, n.d., p. 247.
14. B.B. Goswami, op. cit., p. 131.
15. Ibid.
16. A. McDonald, Memo No. 10772/1873 G of 13-1-1946, cited in R.S. Samuelson, op. cit., p. 34.

17. Khawtinkhuma and Vanthuama, *Mizo Union Mite Hnena Thuchah*, Aizawl, 1947, p. 2. Cited in ibid., p. 35.
18. Ibid.
19. Hariathirna (Public Notice) by McDonald, Memo No. 10772–1873 G of 13-1p1-1946 cited in ibid., p. 36.
20. B.B. Goswami, op. cit., p. 132.
21. Vanlawma, *Kan Ram etc*, op. cit., p. 111.
22. Bimal J. Dev and Dilip K. Lahini, *Manipur Culture and Politics*, Delhi, 1987, pp. 100–101.
23. See N. Lokendra Singh, 'Socio-Economic Roots of Popular Movements in Manipur Valley, Ph.D. thesis, Manipur University, 1990. Also N. Joykumar Singh, *Social Movements in Manipur*, New Delhi, 1992.
24. Ibid.
25. Ibid., pp. 236–242.
26. Ibid.
27. Ibid.
28. Ibid.
29. Ibid.
30. Ibid., pp. 242–43.
31. Laldena, 'The INA Movement' in Laldena, G. Kabui, Joykumar Singh, *History of Modern Manipur*, Imphal, 1991, pp. 174–82.
32. Ibid.
33. Ibid.
34. Ibid.
35. Ibid.
36. Ibid.
37. Joykumar Singh, 'Movement for Responsible Government in India (1938–48)', in *Proceedings of the North East India History Association*, Barapani Session, 1983, pp. 202–209. Also his *Social Movements in Manipur*, New Delhi, 1992.
38. Ibid.
39. Ibid.
40. Ibid.
41. Ibid.
42. Ibid.
43. Ibid.
44. Ibid.
45. Ibid.
46. Ibid.
47. Nehru to T. Sakhrie cited in *National Herald*, 6th August, 1946.
48. Vumson, op. cit., p. 248.
49. B.B. Goswami, op. cit., p. 134. More detials in the Chapter V.
50. Vumson, op. cit., p. 249. Also Vanlawma, *Kan Ram etc.* op. cit., p. 119. This and the following discussion and verbal agreement between the two could not be confirmed from any other sources.
51. Ibid.
52. Vanlawma, Ibid., p. 119.
53. Ibid.
54. Ibid.

55. Vumson, op. cit. Also Ibid.
56. Ibid.
57. Vumson,.op. cit. Also Ibid.
58. Ibid.
59. Ibid., p. 136. Vumson, op. cit., p. 252. Also, B.B. Goswami, op. cit., p. 138.
60. Ibid.
61. Ibid.
62. Vanlawma, *Kan Ram etc.*, op. cit., p. 119.
63. Ibid.
64. Ibid.
65. Ibid.
66. Ibid., p. 122.
67. Ibid.
68. Ibid., p. 124.
69. Asoso Yonuo, op. cit., p. 166.
70. Ibid.
71. Ibid.
72. *Naga Nation*, February 1947.
73. Cited in Asoso Yonou, op. cit., p. 169. Also see V. Venkata Rao, et al., *Century of Government and Politics in North-East India*, Vol. III, Mizoram, New Delhi, 1987, pp. 38–39.

CHAPTER FOUR

STATE OF MIND

The period proved to be the most crucial juncture of history for the Naga, Mizo and the Meitheis of North East India. The structure of their new consciousness and the socio-political process of mobilisation had immense repercussion on the state of their minds. It generated different types of feeling among different people. For the Nagas the emerging situation generated extreme fear that shifted to Indian hegemony, they would not be able to perpetuate the reproduction of their social, cultural and biological systems and whatever they had been able to establish by this time would also be taken away. For the Mizos on the other hand the situation generated hope that now they had the option to live under a social democratic regime. The Meitheis were suspicious and apprehensive about the Indians and what kind of rule it would introduce in Manipur. These sets of fear, apprehensions and hope were the deciding factor as far as the question of their respective integration with India was concerned. Eventually these state of minds decided the shape of history of the region and that of India in north east India. While the Mizos overwhelmingly opted for India, the Nagas preferred an independent existence. A weak stream of thinking still was against severance of all ties with India at that point. But the clues found in the Constitution of Burma adopted by the National Government of Burma in 1947 were adopted. This Constitution provided for the Right of Secession for the Burmese minorities after a period of ten years of experimentation with the Burmese rule. Thus the Nagas also insisted on a ten year experimentation period with India which was agreed upon in the NNC-Akbar Hydari Agreement. But the difference of opinion regarding the interpretation of the clause which embodied this condition led to the failure of pact. The Meitheis had little trepidation identifying themselves with Indian civilisation but they were apprehensive of the exact nature of prospective Indian rule and its impact on the socio-economic life of Manipur. Their experience was bitter. So they needed time to get rid of the apprehension. But the Indian post-colonial State neither provided them that time nor appreciated their crisis. The manner in which it hurriedly pushed through the merger only succeeded in alienating the Meitheis more. It was apparent that the Post colonial Indian state was only interested in absorption of their territory, not seek or respect the democratic opinion of the people.

In the following pages we discuss the nature of hope, fear and apprehension experienced by the people on the eve of their incorporation in the Indian state.

The Fear

Nagas were not the same people in the forties of the twentieth century whom the British had conquered in the later half of the nineteenth century. Great changes had taken place since then. The First World War blew strong winds across Nagaland in terms of ideas and images. There was the battle of Kohima against the Japanese in the Second World War. The Nagas not only saw the war but experienced the ravages. They worked as helpers and porters to the British army. The head-hunting Nagas accustomed to tribal warfares actually witnessed a modern warfare. Then there were the Naga soldiers who formed part of the British army returning home from overseas after the war. There were refugees trekking from Burma to India through Nagaland. Close to it came the imminence of British withdrawal; Separatist claims of the Muslims and Sikhs and the prospective partition of India. There were questions regarding the future of the Princely States and tribals areas.

The Nagas were, to use T. Aliba Imti's words, "at the most critical time of their history. They were neither sure of their identity nor their future."[1] There was a great debate going on among the educated Nagas over their identity — whether they were Indians or not? Do they form a part of India or not.[2] The long years of protective exclusion from India and Indians had inhibited them from identifying with India. At the same time they formed a part of British India. What they were sure was that India consisted of people who even though heterogeneous themselves, were distinctly different from the Nagas in terms of society and culture. The backward Nagas were no political match to them. So there was every possibility that thrown among forty crores of Indians the one million Nagas with their unique system of life will be wiped out.[3] This 'unique system of life' was dearest to the Nagas and they desired its perpetuation. While this desire formed the core of the Naga popular perception of 'independence', 'sovereignty' to them meant to be 'left alone', to live life in the inherited and accustomed way — however crude and uncivilized it might seem to others, whereas joining India might mean a "threat to their old way of life, their freedom, their valued traditions, their customary laws, their land (and mystic mountain homes), their freedom."[4] They were apprehensive that as soon as they became a part of India, their socio-economic life would be interfered with, an alien administrative set up, taxes imposed, and development according to peoples' own free will would be impeded. They feared the rule of people who had no knowledge about the Nagas. They had made these fears, apprehensions and paranoia clear to the British Government as well as Indian leadership repeatedly in the Memoranda submitted to the Statutory Commission in 1929 and to the Constituent Assembly. At the same time they were not in favour of instant severance of all ties with India. T. Aliba Imti felt it would be 'unwise' for the Nagas to cut itself off from India at that stage.[5] The Nagas could press for 'protection' against the fears and apprehensions and secure 'Home Rule' under Indian administration. Since the debate over the identity and future of the Nagas was still on and the fear of alien rule still persisted, the Naga elite wanted time so that the Nagas could resolve the issues themselves. They wanted a ten year interim arrangement at the end of which the option would be open to the Nagas. Till then they wanted a political state conducive to the perpetuation of 'Nagaism' — the Naga way of life. But despite the initial agreement, the Government of India backed out and refused to leave the options open for the Nagas at the expiry of the ten years term.

An instance of the Naga image of independence was provided by T. Sakhrie, the NNC Secretary wherein he clearly stated the life the Nagas feared to lose:

> In the life of the village the family is a permanent living institution, a conscious unit in the national polity. Every family is proud of its own and no family has ever been left by their fellowmen to the mercy of circumstances. Possessing his own house, built on his own land, no family ever pays tax. Forests, woodlands and rivers belong to the people for their exploitation without paying taxes. We cultivate as much land as we need and there is no one to question our rights. We have food to eat and drinks to drink exceedingly above our needs. Truly God has been good to us. Three square meals a day and Zu (rice beer) without measure. We have no beggars. It has no landlords to harass it and no revenue collectors to knock on its doors. For the family is the master of its own affairs and wonder of wonders we have no jail. We do not arrest nor ever imprison anyone. Our civil authority is God in the matter of life and death. We fear nobody, individually and collectively. We are a healthy people and fear corrupts the health of men. What peace we have. No police, no CID. We have no locks. Our granaries are kept outside the village and no guard is needed for there is no one to steal from them. We travel as we like and it costs us nothing. If by ill-fortune a man falls sick or dies, he is brought home to his family without counting the costs. We talk freely, live freely and often fight freely too. There is order in this chaos. If I were to choose a country, it would be Nagaland, my fair Nagaland again and again.[6]

The Nagas had a 'shrewd suspicion' that there was conspiracy to take away from them — this freedom of 'living freely, talking freely, and fighting freely.' Becoming a part of India was presented to them as 'imposition of an alien culture and administration' which would mean a loss of their land and this freedom. It is said that the 'Naga love for his ancestral home and fields is so great that the slightest suspicion regarding its safety drove him to destruction. During the pre-accession period, the fear of loss of land, freedom and Indianisation were harped on continuously so effectively that it became a part of their psyche.

> "The tillers of soil who had grown and lived on the land know the previous value of the land to which they are affectionately attached. Living their lives in the mystic mountain houses, the villagers felt a threat to their old way of life, their freedom, their valued traditions, their customary laws, their land, their freedom and everything that was theirs but begin to wonder if in the changing context of things, it would be possible anymore."[7]

While discussing the Simon Commission proposals for Naga hills in the House of Commons (May 1935) one of the members of the house, Mr. Cadogan, who had conversation with the Nagas in the Naga hills, said that these hillmen 'resent' even the 'slightest suspicion that something is being done to take away from them their immemorial rights and customs.'[8] There was also a stronger lurking apprehension in the tribal minds that the teeming masses of Indian plainsmen would overflow their habitat, disrupting their traditional way of life and depriving them of their most precious possession — their lands. The tribals did not possess anything in terms of material assets and were therefore all the more fanatically attached to their land which provided him and his family with their essential sources of sustenance year after year. Therefore, if the British were leaving, the Nagas were not ready to let anyone else into their land to rule over them.[9] The Naga perception of freedom has to be understood within this context.

The Hope

Unlike Nagas, the Mizos (Lushais) were not direct participants in the Second World War. But on the other side of the border, in Burma, their brethren did go through the war. Tiddim, one of the main towns of Burma inhabited by the Chins to which the Lushais belonged, was occupied by the combined Japanese-INA army. Although only a few Mizos joined the Japanese army despite invokations, the Chins referred to the Japanese as *to thak* or new masters.[10] Thus they too felt the winds of change. The closeness of the Japanese troops and the political enslavement of the Mizo people at the hands of the British Superintendent and their own Mizo Chiefs fostered political consciousness in these hills. Faint news of the nationalist struggle for independence being waged in the plains under the leadership of Mahatma Gandhi in this side of the frontier and Aung San in the other kept filtering through the sieves of the British censorships. The erstwhile apolitical tribals now began to be apprehensive about their future. Those living close to Burma felt that they would be attached to Burma while those who lived in Assam wished that they would be left alone.[11] They had no idea of the emergence of modern India or Burmese nation. They merely wanted to live with their own people. International demarcation of borders so far meant nothing to them. It was their ethnicity that mattered. But the educated among them knew it was time to make decisions. Education had already opened the windows of the world to the few educated Mizos. The ex-servicemen coming back home after the war also related new ideas and experiences. This new outlook influenced the Mizo perception of independence which was in turn determined by an immediate problem the Mizo populace was facing — it was the damning the Chiefly rule. From the time the Sailos' assumed chieftainship Mizos were reeling under their oppressive rule. The theoretically egalitarian society was virtually polarised into two loose classes of people, the chiefs, the upas (close advisors) and their favorites on the one hand and the commoners on the other. The chiefs generally functioned like autocratic rulers treating common people as personal servants and slaves. They were entitled to a number of customary taxes. They were paid *fathang* or taxes in kind out of the total individual share of paddy, *Sachchiah* or the best honey obtained. Besides these, people had to pool their labour to construct the chiefs house whenever summoned to do so. The situation was amply recorded in the Mizo folk song:[12]

Bai thak arva
artui khawn leh lal hnugvi rengkaning tawh
kawlu chawi lal daltu an ni sazai hian pui an ni

(We have had enough of Chief's rule. He orders us to do all his works which we have to do. He demands eggs and chickens frequently from us which we cannot refuse. We always have to carry out his orders and in the process get late for our own works. Alas! this is indeed a severe punishment.)

There are many other such folksongs which expressed similar grievances against the oppressive rule of the Chiefs. Suffice it to say here that the Chief's office had ample opportunities to practise corruption and indeed they did. They took bribe (ramhual) from villagers who wanted to be alloted best plots of land. The chiefs also had their own favourites who were granted special favour at the cost of the commoners. The Lushais had risen in a massive widespread revolt against the chiefs just before the advent of the English (circa 1840) which failed.[13] The British recognition of the office of chieftainship not only perpetuated the chief's rule, it was in fact strengthened. Under the colonial protection the chiefs began to abuse their power and authority. The immediate issue before the Mizos from then onwards was to get rid of the chiefs. The situation was complicated by the emergence of a feeble educated Mizo intelligentsia which sought recognition as the Mizo elite. This was resented by the chiefs who were not only the traditional elite but was also recognised as such by the British.

The imminent withdrawal of the British from India provided a hopeful opportunity to secure the abolition of chieftainship. The Mizo commoners were optimistic that they could secure an assurance to this effect from the Indian National Congress and merge with India on this condition. For the Mizos the fear was the continuation of the chief's rule which they wanted to halt even at the cost of losing their sovereignty.

The Apprehension

Even though Mongoloid and Tibeto-Burman speaking, the Meitheis were different from the Nagas and Mizos. Hinduism was the State religion in Manipur from the eighteenth century. Even though imposed from above, Hinduism soon established a stronghold. Within a century, there was a rudimentary caste system in operation, dominance of Brahmins and social exclusion of the tribals from the Hindu society. At the same time, it blended well with the pre-Hindu semi-tribal structure producing a synthesised Hinduism. The Meitheis, specially the dominant 'Kshyatriyas' and the 'Brhamins' who surprisingly were a numerous section of the population took pride in being a Hindu and a constituent of the Indian civilization.

Manipur also has a rich history of social and political movements. Colonial rule and the consequent socio-economic transformation of Manipur destablished the closed up society and created quite a few tensions in the structure. The anti-colonial resistance movement led by Tkendrajit Singh did not end with his execution. It had filtered down to the masses. This popular unrest against the British entry into Manipur and its colonial regime continued till the 1940s. The Kuki Rebellion (1917-20) and the Movement under Jadonang and Gaidinliu (1930-49) were part of this unrest and attempts to shake off the oppressive regime. Then there was a movement against the abolition of slavery and lallup (1892) followed by the Bazar Boycott agitation (1920) and anti-Potang Agitation (1909–11). This was followed by the Nupilan Movement (first phase–1904, second phase — 1939-40)-Sanamahi Movement (1930) State Peoples' Movement for Responsible Government (1946–48) and the Communist Movement (1948-50) attempting a Telengana-like uprising. Among these, the Bazar Boycott agitation, the Sanamahi movement and the Nupilan movement though results of local conditions, had serious implications as far as the shaping of the anti-Indian attitude was concerned.

Alongwith the British, it was the Marwaris, and the Sikh merchants cum moneylenders who entered Manipur and monopolised the trade and mercantile practice. Often they would buy up all the rice produced in Imphal valley for export. This often created severe shortage for local consumption. The War time export during both first and second global wars by the Marwari (who were called Mayangs by the Meitheis) traders succeeded in creating a crisis and famine condition in Manipur. The sheer severity of the situation prompted the women folk of Manipur to organise and lead an all-women movement protesting against the export of local rice by outside traders. The movement is known as the Nupilan Movement (1939-40). This successful movement created an image of Indian Businessmen and traders as 'unscrupulous people'. The continuation of such practice by the Marwari traders despite protest movements and social exclusion only reinforced the negative image of Indians in the Meithei mind.

Another significant development took place in the 1930s in Cachar where a sizable Meithei population lived. The rejection, socio-religious obstracisation, and reproachfulness towards the Meithei Hindus by the Bengali caste Hindus made the Meithei community reject Hinduism and revert to their former animist religion called 'Sanamahi'. Thus the Sanamahi Movement was an effort to reject Hinduism and embrace back the Sanamahi cult. Though the movement was not successful then (it was a huge success in the 1970s) it made people aware of their pre-Hindu roots as well as the possibility of rejection as Hindus by the vanguards of mainstream Hinduism. Thus an image of India as a hostile cultural, economic and political system and Indians as part of the system was slowly being built in the popular mind. The Meithei mind had slowly begun to have misgivings and apprehensions about India. The image of the exploitative Marwari businessmen loomed large in his vision whenever he thought of India and Indians about whom he had very little idea.

Manipur was one of the first states where a State Peoples' Movement against Princely autocracy and in favour of a popular government was launched. Prolonged struggle under the leadership of Hizam Irabat had succeeded in installing an elected state Assembly. The release from a claustrophobic autocracy and peoples' victory was celebrated with festivity but it was short-lived.

REFERENCES

1. T. Aliba Imti, *Reminiscences: From Impur to Naga National Council*, Mokokchung, 1988, pp. 27–28
2. Ibid.
3. Naga National Council Memorandum to His Majesty's Government and the Government of India, 20 February, 1947.
4. Ibid.
5. T. Aliba Imti, Secretary, Naga National Council, Public Address Kohima, 6 December, 1946.
6. T. Sakhrie, cited in Verrier Elwin, Nagaland, Shillong, 1961, pp. 73–75.
7. Ibid.
8. Verrier Elwin, op. cit, pp. 36–37
9. Nari Rustomji, *Imperilled Frontier*, OUP, 1989, p. 29
10. Nirmal Nibedan, *Mizoram the Dagger Brigade*, New Delhi, 1980, pp. 71–72.
11. Ibid.
12. Thanpuii Pa, Mizo Hla (Mizo Songs) in R. Sena Samuelson, Love Mizoram, Imphal, 1985, p. 54.
13. Sankhima, *A Mizo Uprising,* Proceedings of the North East India History Association, 1989 (Session), pp. 200–205.

CHAPTER FIVE

POLITICS OF INTEGRATION

The impending freedom of India with Partition also signalled the demise of the Indian princely states. For the 562 States occupying almost two-fifth of the subcontinent the rush of events that precipitated the dissolution of the raj was abrupt. For almost a century, the Princes had been encouraged to regard themselves as a bulwark of stability in India and various strategies had been devised by the raj to shove up their position in the face of the corrosive impact of nationalism.[1] However, when the moment came for the raj to bow out of the Indian stage, it failed to ensure the continued survival of the Princely states.[2] The Cabinet Mission had laid down that with India's independence the doctrine of paramountcy would lapse and that the states could negotiate terms with the successor government in which they could constitute a power block alongside the Hindu and Muslim group of provinces. Many states welcomed the idea; some even set up a committee to negotiate the terms with the Indian parties.[3] However, discords between the Congress and League and the hostility of the Congress towards the pretension of the princes saw little progress being achieved.[4] What precipitated matters was the Partition Plan of 3rd June.[5] While the plan affirmed that paramountcy would lapse, it frankly discounted the rights of states to declare its independence through a federation of states or becoming dominions on an individual basis. With the concurrence of the Congress and the League, Mountbatten set up two State Departments to resolve the problem of the accession of states.[6] At the suggestion of Patel the Congress devised a formula which required the states to accede to India by ceding certain subjects in which the common interest of the country was involved.[7] In other matters, pledged Patel, "we would scrupulously respect their continuous existence."[8] Some of the princes knew that the die had been cast and had resigned to their respective fate while in others the State People's Movement for responsible government had also indicated their future.[9] The more ambitious rulers or dewans of states like Hyderabad, Bhopal and Travancore were dreaming of an independence which would keep them as autocratic as before and such hopes received considerable encouragement from the Government of India's Political Department under Conrad Corfield till Mountbatten enforced a more strict policy.[10] The imminent declaration of independence by Hyderabad, Bhopal and Travancore would unleash yet another serious crisis setting examples to other states. Mountbatten could clearly see this prospect.[11] Hence he hastily summoned a conference of Princes in late July, where he used his persuasion to get the princes to sign the Instrument of Accession highlighting the advantages that these terms gave to princes and warning that failing to do so before 15 August would leave the princes without an outside mediator to argue on their behalf.[12] Whatever resistance there was among the princes seemed to have crumbled at this point and by 15 August almost all had signed the Instrument of Accession except for Hyderabad, Kashmir, Junagadh, Tripura and Manipur.[13] In doing so some of these princes were influenced by the political developments in their respective states because meanwhile a new upsurge of State Peoples' Movement for responsible government had erupted in those states. These movement were anti-monarchial, anti-feudal and pan-Indian in character.

The non-Malayalee citizens of south Travancore were disgusted with the oppressive rule of the Malayalee Maharaja of Travancore and directed their anger against the Malayalee community.[14] On the basis of this situation the ambitious Dewan of this princely state launched a move for an independent Travancore and Cochin movement and declared its intention of not joining the Indian Union. It came out with an American model of constitution to be adopted for itself. The communist activists, who had build a very powerful base among the coir factory workers, fishermen, toddy-tappers and agricultural labourers employed by the Jemmi landlords, launched a massive campaign against this conspiracy. The police repression was followed by the rebels acquiring military training for self-defence. There was a violent confrontation between the state and the rebels in Punnapra and Vayalar in which at least eight hundred people were massacred by the police. This event coincided with the ongoing Akhila Kerala movement which had been working for the formation of a multilingual Kerala state which would include Travancore and Cochin.[15] The movement was a joint venture of the Kerala Pradesh Congress Committee, Travancore State Congress and Cochin Praja Mandalam which had the support of the Maharaja of Cochin too. The hostility against the Travancore royalty consequent to the brutal suppression of the Punnapra-Vayalar movement strengthened the anti-monarchial state of the movement and attracted mass support for the unification of Kerala and its integration with the Indian union. Even though the Royalty tried to back out and seek to retain its autocracy, the Punnapra-Valayar and Akhila Kerala movement prevented a possible secessionism and facilitated the merger of Travancore-Cochin with the Union.[16]

July 1946 to October 1951 saw the rise of another massive communist led peasant insurgency in the Telengana region of Hyderabad state, where a small Urdu speaking Muslim elite had a religio-linguistic hegemony over the majority of Telegu speaking people.[17] There was a total violation of political and civil liberties and the grossest form of feudal exploitation was perpetrated by Muslims and high caste Hindu Deshmukh landlord and Jagirdars who extorted *Vetti* (forced labour) from the peasants and retained bonded labourers through a debt-trap. While the ambitious Nizam was conspiring to set up an independent state and not join the Indian union the peasants broke out in revolt. The bloody guerilla warfare of the peasants against the ruthless *razakar* army of the Nizam lasted a long time and succeeded in establishing several independent pockets in the region. This anti-Nizam movement brought about the collapse of the autocratic regime of India's biggest princely state when the Indian army entered the scene and paved the way for the integration of Hyderabad with Indian Union. The movement of the Andhra Mahasabha for separation from Madras and the formation of a separate Telengana province also had contributed immensely to the integration. The pan-Indian character of the Telengana uprising was evident in the fact that the adoption of the slogan of overthrowing the new Indian government had little appeal to the masses.[18]

The progressive National Conference of Sheikh Abdulla had launched a 'Quit Kashmir' movement against the very unpopular and despotic Hindu Maharaja of the Muslim majority state of Kashmir.[19] When Sheikh Abdulla was arrested on 20th May while leading the movement, Nehru rushed to the support of the Kashmiri leader and was even arrested for defying the ban on his entry to Kashmir. Soon after this negotiations with Kashmir's prime minister Kak began for a possible accession of Kashmir into India; Nehru agreed to protect 'Kashmiriat' — the identity of Kashmir, assured them of Article 370 which would allow Kashmir to have a special status in the Union of having its own legislature, non-transferability of land to non-Kashmiris etc. At the prospect of losing Kashmir the raiders from Pakistan invaded Kashmir which hastened the entry of Indian army and effected the accession of Kashmir into the Union, though almost half of it was occupied by the Pakistan raiders. This altered the whole outlook for the states. Bhopal joined the Union. Nehru who presided over the Gwalior session of the All India State Peoples' Conference (April 1947) warned that the states refusing to join the Constituent Assembly would be treated as hostile. Along with such verbal threats came promises too. Patel assured the princes "The Congress are no enemies of the Princely Order, but on the other hand wish them and the people under the aegis all prosperity, contentment and happiness."[20] While Bhawalpur succeeded in joining Pakistan Junagadh did not. The Eastern States Union formed by recalcitrant princes crumbled in December 1947 in the face of powerful prajamandal agitations in Nilgiri, Dhankanal and Talcher in Orissa.[21] Junagadh's Muslim ruler in Kathiawad tried to join Pakistan but his attempt was thwarted by popular agitation coupled with Indian police action.[22] The Congress exceptionally strong in Mysore since the late 1930s, launched a fairly uninhibited 'Mysore Chalo' agitation on its own in September 1947, which forced substantial political changes in a democratic direction by 12 October.[22] By then, most of the states agreed to sign the Instrument of Accession to join the Indian Union acknowledging central authority of the centre over defence, external affairs and communication. The princes agreed to this fairly easily because they surrendered only what they did not have all this time and there was no change in the internal political structures yet. The myriad small states were merged with the neighbouring units to form unions like Kathiawad union, Vindhya and Madhyapradesh, Rajasthan or Himachal Pradesh while princes were made happy with the bait of a fat privy purse, some of them were made Governors or Rajpramukhs.[23]

As far as North-east India was concerned, partition had devastated the region economically, politically and culturally. Following the prospect of abolition of chieftain-ship, the oppressed Mizos of the Lushai hills were inclined to join India while the Nagas wanted a ten years period of experience of Interim government after which they would decide their future. Manipur had an assembly constituted by people's representative after a long struggle for responsible government, but the communist-phobia that had gripped the Indian state following Telengana, Punnapra-Valyalar, (Tebhaga in) Bengal, Tripura, Maharashtra, Punjab and Tamilnadu proved fateful. In fact by the end of the war the CPI was in a position to claim to be the third biggest party after Congress and League and obviously weaker than them.[24] The inexplicable fear of communism was compounded by the world wide spectre too — especially the events in China and Burma which bordered north-east. Home Minister Patel wanted to ban the party.[25] The Assam chief minister Bordoloi was willing to allow autonomy to

Manipur so that it did not affect Assam.[26] The communists were trying to organise a Telengana-like uprising in Manipur which sealed the fate of this princely state.[27] The neighbouring Tripura was already witnessing a similar uprising. The seize of Manipur became essential to stop the march of communism into the mainland of India.

Naga Hills

The appeal of the Nagas failed to convince the British Labour Government as Naga hills and Naga areas were always considered a part of British India and were administered as such by the government. This was despite the fact that some British civil servants regarded that the tribals of north east were not really Indians. Racially, culturally and otherwise they were projected as non-Indians even though they formed a part of British India. That is why plans of some local administrators to retain the control of some of these areas under the plan of Crown-Colony or Trust Territory were not favoured by the government. Moreover, the Labour Government which had already decided on a complete withdrawal did not want to open up another ponderous issue at such a critical juncture. Therefore, the government maintained complete silence on the Memorandum of the Nagas. The Memorandum sent by the NNC to the British Prime Minister which sought to 'present the case of the Naga people for self determination' urged "His Majesty's Government and the Government of India to set up an Interim Government for a period of ten years, at the end of which the Naga people will be left to choose any form of Government under which they will live." The receipt of this Memorandum was not acknowledged by the Secretary of State for India officially. But in a private top secret letter to Mountbatten, Sir Pethick Lawrence acknowledged its receipt and transfer to Sir Henry Knight.[28] It was felt that the Memorandum need not be taken seriously as NNC was a self constituted body and not representative of all Nagas. It presented only the educated Nagas and not the traditional elders of the village. Knight felt that the underlying thrust of the Memorandum was not political but the preservation of the economic equilibrium of the Naga hills until the Nagas were educated enough to be able to compete with the free and independent Indian voters. This could be attained only by some form of Interim Self Government. Mere incorporation of Naga hills in Assam might lead to the collapse of the Naga economy resulting in famines and to the relapse of the Nagas into head hunting isolation.

Mountbatten in another private letter mentioned that he had clarified from the Assam Governor, Andrew Clow that although NNC was indeed a self constituted body it did have a representative character. He agreed that the Interim government had to be a continuation of British rule. To put the Nagas under a Central Indian Government would mean the subjection of the tribes to the politicians of Delhi who would be more unaware of their needs than the Assam administrators. But if the tribals could be ensured some suitable safeguards within the framework of Indian Constitution, they could themselves expect some share in the Government and would have access and influence over the Government. The main hurdle was that these tribal areas were deficit areas and would need the support of other province. The thrust should be to ensure the protection of the tribals from exploitation and the preservation of their way of living.[29]

When the Prime Minister Lord Attlee had to reply to a question of Sir Walter Smiles on the Nagas' demand for an interim arrangement it was pointed out that Nagas should submit their problems to the Advisory Committee on Tribal Areas of the Constituent Assembly. In other words the government transferred the matter to the Indian leadership. What Andrew Clow (Feb. 1947) told the Nagas was part of this policy only. In a philosophical manner he advised the Nagas to reach an understanding and be accommodative with the people of the plains for their own benefit.[30] They should not think only in terms of what they could get but also what they could give. The Nagas who lived life in pure democracy could share of a lot their experience with the plain people and receive the benefit of development and progress from the Indian administration in reciprocation. The Deputy Commissioner of Naga hills, Pawsey by now found that things were not working in his favour and Nagas were being obstinate in their demand for a sovereign Nagaland. He tried to remind the Nagas that they were still primitive and naked people forming a sullen minority of the subcontinent. As such the need of the hour was to remain united. He said:

> "Changes in the Government of India are on their way and the Naga hills too will experience changes. Fortunately here, there is no communal trouble and we shall be spared of the bloodshed of Calcutta, Noakhali, Bihar and Punjab and if Nagas remain united, they will be able not only to administer themselves in a peaceful atmosphere but also will be able, through unity, to influence the adjoining areas where strife is prevalent. At as costs Nagas must remain united."[31]

But the new found enthusiasm and the prospect of ruling a sovereign Nagaland made the Naga elite obstinate. They not only refused to give up their stance, they even encouraged the Mizos, Meitheis and the Assamese, to declare themselves independent to strengthen their case. In a statement issued on 21st May 1947, the Naga leaders called upon the Assamese, not to join the Indian Union, but form an independent Assam and work in cooperation with the federal Naga State. It continued,

> "The Nagas who were determined not to allow themselves to be involved in a divided and chaotic India, are prepared to declare their own independence and can think of entering into a ten-year treaty with an independent Assam."[32]

Amidst all these, the sub-committee on the future administration of the tribal and excluded areas, under the chairmanship of Gopinath Bordoloi, constituted under the aegis of the Committee on Aboriginal Tribes under the chairmanship of Sardar Patel (under the Constituent Assembly constituted in November 1946) visited Kohima on 27 May 1947 to find out the wishes of the Nagas. In his welcome address to the sub-committee, T. Sakhrie the Secretary of the NNC said,

"You have come to find out from us, the desire of the Naga people on the question of how their land should be governed when the British power withdraws from India. I am sure the members of NNC who are all present in this house will make your task easy, in that Nagas are invisible and have one voice, I hope you will do all in your power to help the Nagas achieve their demand."

The NNC then put forward that:

1. The Nagas want autonomous status under the guardianship of India for ten years, at the expiry of which they would be free to decide their future.
2. The Interim government of the Naga people will rule over the people of Nagaland having full powers in respect of legislation, executive and judiciary.
3. Nagaland belongs to Naga people and will be inalienable.
4. The interim government of the Naga people will have full powers in matters of raising revenue and expenditure, an annual subvension to cover the deficit being given by the guardian power.
5. For defence and aiding civil power in case of emergency a force considered necessary by the Naga National Council will be maintained in Nagaland by the Guardian Power.[33]

Bardoloi however was not convinced of the demand.[32] He tried to impress upon the members of the NNC, the necessity and benefits of Naga hills in remaining a part of India. On the issue of evolving a device to integrate the administration of the hill people with those of the plains, and taking into consideration the fear, apprehensions and demands of the Naga people, Bardoloi recommended in his report that "All the tribes of provinces other than Assam should be treated as a minority. As regards Assam, conditions in the hill districts in which Naga hills, the Lushai hills and North Cachar hills have been included are on a totally different footing and the atmosphere, partially in the excluded areas is one which is not to be found elsewhere. These areas must therefore be treated separately from the rest."[34]

The committee then went on to lay down a number of provisions for the Tribal and Excluded Areas of Assam. These recommendations subsequently formed the provisions of the Fifth and Sixth Schedules of the Indian constitution.

On the failure of the mission of the Advisory Committee to arrive at any agreement with the Nagas on the future constitutional set up, Sri Akbar Hydari, ICS, the Indian Governor of Assam who succeeded Andrew Clow was sent to Kohima on 26th June 1947 to impress upon the Nagas to understand the realities of the situation and negotiate with them to come to an agreement and merge with India. In his welcome address to Hydari, T. Sakhrie, the secretary of the NNC said:

> As is known to your Excellency, the Naga people have submitted a Memorandum to His Majesty's Government and the Government of India asserting their rights for self determination and demanding the setting up of an Interim Government. Of the Naga people for a period of ten years, so as to enable the Nagas to be so schooled so as to make a responsible choice at the end of ten years. Apart from the reply given by the Prime Minister of England to a question of Sir Walter Smiles, seen in the Newspaper columns, no reply to this memorandum of the Naga people have been received. The Naga National Council still looks for a reply and reiterates the statement made in the Memorandum that 'A constitution drawn by people who have no knowledge of Nagaland and the people will be quite unacceptable to the Naga people.' It is our desire to make it plain to your Excellency that it will not be enough to say in the end that a constitution has been drawn upon the lines suggested by the Cabinet Mission. We know that your Excellency will concede that the Naga people have as much right for self determination as any other people. Our request to your Excellency is to do all that is in your power to enable the Nagas to stand on their own feet, so that they may be worthy members of a civilized world.[35]

After a series of hectic meetings and discussions with the members of the NNC and the Deputy Commissioner Pawsey for three days — 27, 28, and 29 June 1947 — on the question of the ten years Interim demand put forward by the Naga leaders, Governor Hydari expressed his full sympathy for the legitimate rights of the Naga people to an honourable life and worked on a compromise formula known as the Hydari Agreement comprising nine points with full consent of Nehru and Bordoloi.[36] The Agreement recognised the rights of the Nagas to develop themselves according to their free wishes. The Naga Government would be given full legislative, executive and judicial power as far as Naga people were concerned and like Kashmir legislation passed in Central or provincial legislatives would not be effective on the Nagas. While the Naga Government will be responsible for the imposition, collection and expenditure of taxes, if at all, the Naga lands and its other resources could not be alienated to a non-Naga. The clause nine of the agreement specified that "The Governor of Assam as the Agent of the Government of the Indian Union will have a special responsibility for a period of ten years to ensure the observance of this agreement; at the end of this period, the Naga National Council will be asked whether they require the above Agreement to be extended for a further period or a new agreement regarding the future of the Naga people arrived at."

Clause Nine was formulated and agreed to after a lot of discussion. This needs to be elaborated because subsequently this particular clause sealed the fate of the agreement. Narrating the events, Aliba Imti wrote in his Memoir:

> The (first days) discussion went on freely and with open-hearted attitude from both sides without any reservation. The first days meeting ended at 5 O'clock. Next *morning the meeting's discussion was (sic) centered on* the word **Interim** and bit by bit the discussion progressed. The afternoon session was very tricky. On many occasions we put the Governor in a very tight corner. The Governor left the meeting at 5 P.M. requesting us to let him know the same evening whether NNC would agree to his amendment. The members' discussion con-

tinued upto 8 P.M. and the burden of going down to the Governor's camp with the discussion of NNC, was given to me. I invited some of the senior members to accompany me at least for physical support while meeting the Governor, but they preferred to send me alone.

The Governor and the DC were sitting in the Governor's camp and they looked at me with expectant eyes. To avoid an awkward situation I quickly told them 'Sorry Sirs'. Pointing out a chair to me the Governor said, "Sit down Mr. Imti." At his request I gave a short summary about the discussion, He said, "Alright I am contacting New Delhi immediately and shall inform your decision to the Prime Minister." Next morning he came up with a new proposal on the last point. The Governor's proposal on the very controversial point No. 9 was as follows:

"That at the end of 10 years Nagas will be free to choose any form of Government provided they did not join Pakistan or Burma."

The whole meeting was spent only on this 9th point modification and we refused to change even a word of our decision. As it will be understood that the NNC wanted absolute freedom to chose their Government after 10 years and the Government of India may not be ready to that extent. The afternoon session continued and we came to an agreement with all the 9 points (with modification) of our original demands. The last modification of point 9 according to me was less effective than that of Governor's proposal. But I was amused with certain reservation that how the members quite willingly accepted the last proposal from the Governor, that the proposal was something like this that at the end of 10 years, the NNC or the Government in power at that time shall be asked by the Government . . .(etc.)' And as such the famous 10 years Interim Government was made and the term of the agreement was signed by the Governor of Assam and myself on behalf of the NNC. We made three copies, Governor took copies with him

> and one copy remained with the NNC. That evening everybody was happy and since (sic) the Governor had promised us that if we come to an agreement, it would be implemented immediately, say within a month.[37]

It was a triumphant moment for the NNC. Aliba Imti who was the Secretary of NNC declared that:

> The foundation stone of our cherished goal is already laid down let the spirit of difference, if there be any, be taken away from your hearts. Come forward with a united spirit. Let us build a new Nagaland based on the spirit of goodwill and understanding. Let us remember 'Rome was not built in a day' and let us also remember 'United we stand, divided we fall'.[38]

For India too, it was seen as a victory as it was a peaceful step to bring the Nagas into the Union of India by their own will in plain course, so their future was not be chosen outside India.[39] "Akbar Hydari seemed to have accomplished an impossible feat by signing the agreement. He had made his intention clear to the Naga leaders on the same evening of the agreement without any opposition or hostile reaction to it from the NNC leaders by categorically stating to them off the record that 'after the expiry of ten years, the Naga's might change the administrative pattern within India with a view to securing an honourable place but the refusal of which would bring a display of force upon them."[40]

But though both parties went home happy after the agreement, trouble started in their respective headquarters over the 9th clause. There were some problems regarding the interpretation of the clause and despite Akbar Hydari's best effort, the Constituent Assembly refused to rectify the agreement and hence it could not be implemented. Hydari gave the impression that he had Nehru's approval in framing the clause but obviously some interested camps disapproved of the last clause.[41] The NNC leaders suspected it was the Assam Premier Gopinath Bordoloi who wrecked the agreement. In Aliba Imti's words:

> "I believe it was the misfortune of the Nagas that the Governor had to belong to a minority community — a

> Muslim . . . later on we came to learn that the Governor had not been fair and I do not know who was behind/ against the agreement. Was it G.N. Bordoloi or some mysterious hands in New Delhi. The Governor deteriorated (sic)from its original stand."[42]

A similar polarisation took place within the NNC. While the moderates led by Aliba Imti and T. Sakhrie were happy with the outcome the extremists led by Zapu Phizo who had just joined the NNC while analysing the last clause felt it was a sell-out. It now began to find ways to undermine the agreement and began to interpret the last clause as: the Naga had the freedom to opt out of India at the expiry of the stipulated ten years.[43] Deeply influenced by the separatism of the League and its success in carving out Pakistan out of the Indian subcontinent,[44] Phizo accused the NNC leadership of submission to the Indian Union. Phizo wanted a suitable interpretation of clause Nine that Nagas would be independent after the expiry of the ten year period.[45] But the moderates led by T. Sakhrie who were participants in the making of the agreement tried to convince the extremists that so long as the provision of the agreement remains effective the Nagas could maintain their independent life which was guaranteed by the agreement. This 'liberal view' irked Phizo. Thus in a bid to better understand the people, Charles Pawsey, the British D.C., Naga Hill District, stationed at Kohima asked the members of the NNC to put the issue to vote.[46] The pro-agreement Sakhrie group won by a majority while Phizo's group protested that the Hydari Agreement could not be accepted under the present confusion until it guaranteed clearly, the independence of the Nagas after the ten year period. Following this defeat, Phizo withdrew from NNC and formed the People's Independence League for sovereign Nagaland.[47] Phizo toured from village to village to mobilise support in his favour and envisaged the formation of a sovereign Nagaland which would include Naga hills, Tuensang hills, and contiguous Naga areas of Manipur and Burma. He projected his League to be more virulent, more dynamic and purposeful than the moderate NNC. But

Phizo's League could not win much public support. Its following was small and as a political force extremely weak. Inevitably it soon went defunct and Phizo was left with no alternative but return to NNC. But Phizo was soon able to create a lobby within NNC which made the NNC to agree to the interpretation of Phizo of the ninth clause. In early July there was a stormy meeting of the NNC, where the NNC leadership who were instrumental in the making of the agreement were severely attacked and called 'moderates'.

> There was much stormy and heated argument about the Governor's agreement. I (Aliba Imti) was also criticised unfairly. I feel (while criticising me for participating in the subcommittee) my colleagues conveniently forgot that some months before, the NNC had passed a resolution and written to the president and vice-president of the Interim government to include one Naga in the sub-committee. I felt that to defend myself was not as important as to work unitedly in the fast changing pace where we had to work out something solid for the Nagas.[48]

The meeting decided, not unanimously but amidst acrimony, to send a plenipotentiary delegation to New Delhi to seek clarification on the ninth clause and categorically assert that the NNC's interpretation would be that after the expiry of the ten years time the Nagas would be free to declare themselves independent. The makers of the agreement felt it would amount to going back on the agreement but failed to convince the extremist faction. They also felt that the visit at this critical juncture would be impractical.

> . . . but to suddenly send a plenipotentiary delegate to Delhi on the verge of Indian Independence was, I felt impractical. Who to meet in Delhi? Who had the power to give independence to any part of the so called Indian territory I explained to the meeting but they were adamant to send this delegation. I objected and refused to be a member of this delegation." (Aliba Imti even resigned from the post of joint secretary at the end of the meeting)[49]

Nevertheless, a seven-member delegation of the NNC consisting of Phizo, Khrisnisa, Kughato, Kezehol, John Angami, T. Sakhrie and Lhousituo and led by Rev. Longri. Ao was sent to New Delhi. As foreseen by Aliba Imti. The delegation could not meet any of the Interim Government members. The imminent withdrawal of the British, the transfer of power, the issue of partition and the fierce communal riots all around were matters that kept the national leadership on their toes. The hectic political activity seemed to be never-ending. The only alternative seemed to the delegation to meet Gandhi who seemed to be relatively free. The delegation therefore met Gandhi on 19, July 1947 at his Bhangi Colony, New Delhi residence.[50] On being asked to place before Gandhi the purpose of their meeting by the Secretary, the delegation presented before him the history of the Naga people highlighting that the Nagas have never been a part of India including the brief period during which the British conquered them. Even the British kept them 'excluded'. Now that the British withdrawal was 'imminent', the authorities offered them District autonomy. But the Nagas wanted complete independence and they were going to declare independence unilaterally on the 14th August 1947 — a day prior to the Independence of India.

Gandhi reportedly tried to convince the delegation that the foundation of free India was love, brotherhood, non-violence and non-coercion. He promised that once India was free, Nagas like other citizens would be treated with honour.

> Nagas have every right to be independent. We did not want to live under the domination of the British and they are leaving us. I want you to feel that India is yours. I feel that the Naga hills are mine, the matter must stop there. I believe in brotherhood of man but do not believe in force or forced union.[51]

On being told that the Nagas would declare themselves independent on 14th August Gandhi retorted said "Why not now? Why wait for August 14th?" On being told that Sir Akbar Hydari had threatened them with the use of force, on the evening of June 29th 1947, if they dared opt out of India, Gandhi characteristically said:

> "Sir Akbar is wrong. He cannot do that . . . I will come to the Naga hills. I will ask them to shoot me first before one Naga is shot."[52]

The Naga extremist leaders recalled this event after Gandhi was assassinated and carefully made a political use of it from their vantage point in course of a Memorandum submitted to the President of India on 1st November 1957.

> On that historic day, the Naga delegation discussed the affairs of the Nagas fully with the Father of Indian Nation, and they made the Naga position clear to him without ambiguity. What he said was not a sudden impulse of the willingness of the Father of a great Nation trying to be obliging. He was sincere. He saw the undesirable right of the Nagas which should not be violated. We took his word as final as far as Nagaland and India were concerned. Gandhiji interpreted not only his own good nature but it was in full confirmation of the politically and publicly avowed policy of the great Indian National Congress not to be a party to coercion. And in this he was not only upholding the attributed national tradition of India as a country which claims to love not peace alone but 'she had never waged war against any nation'. The glory and pride of India was more important to Gandhiji and thus he laid the corner stone to build-up a greater heritage for future India.[53]

However on their return it was found that the Naga hills were going to be formed as a district of the province of Assam after independence and it would be administered as per the provisions of the Sixth Schedule of the Indian Constitution which was being prepared. The Naga extremists faction campaigned that the Constituent Assembly was not ready to accept the 'Hydari-Agreement' which the NNC had already rejected. This activated the Naga politics with more vigour. It was not only a triumph of the extremist faction of the NNC led by Phizo but it agitated the moderate sections too which participated in the making of the agreement. Their stand was not vindicated and they lost their face. This compelled them to join the extremist line of action and the NNC was under a virtual seize of Phizo who emerged to be a more pragmatic leader. Almost overnight Phizo emerged as the undisputed leader of the Nagas whose suggestions were accepted without much questions while the erstwhile leaders and makers of the NNC like T. Sakhrie and Aliba Imti were relegated to insignificance.[54] What petrified both the faction was that if the Government also rejected the agreement then the Naga future was sealed for ever and whatever option they were given in the Agreement also would not be available to them anymore.

On the eve of the Independence of India the NNC had a two-day meeting on the 13th and 14th August 1947. Aliba Imti was elected the president of NNC and a Council of Action was formed.[55] The council sent a telegram to the Government of India on 14th August 1947 informing that at the end of the ten year period of the Hydari Agreement "the Naga will be free to decide their own future" but which produced no reaction from the government. Another telegram was sent to the UNO that the Nagas did not accept Indian Constitution and at the end of their discussion with India, the Nagas would be independent. The Council asked the Nagas to boycott the celebration of Indian Independence on the 15th August 1947. In the stormy NNC meeting of 13th-14th August representatives of many tribes participated and took part in the meeting to discuss 'whether the Agreement was good or bad.'[56] Mr. Rushukhrie was in the chair and Mr. Kumho was the secretary. The meeting decided that the NNC which stood for the solidarity of the Nagas, should continue to work for the 'good' of the Naga people. It also entrusted a sub-committee comprising of Kevichusa, Mayangnokhcha, Zopianga, Krusiehu, Nchemo, Kezuke and Subongnoklu to draft out a constitution for the future government of Nagaland.[57]

On the morning of 15th August 1947, India was independent. As part of the boycott of the celebration, the Naga boys worked the whole night and made posters and pasted them on the walls, trees and rocks of Kohima. Some of these read "outsiders (Indians) let us separate as friends and live like good neighbours", "Indians, it is better to go from Nagaland without any delay," "Nagaland is for the Nagas", "Naga people want peace".[58] But the Kohima Police which was now a part of the Indian administration of which Nagaland was now a district of the Assam province 'had done a better job by removing almost all the posters before anyone could read them.[59] It became evident that Nagaland was now a part of India.

The Mizo Hills

On 20th February 1947, Clement Attlee announced that the British would leave India by June 1948.[60] The Cabinet Mission had recommended the constitution of Advisory Committee to suggest constitutional devices to protect the right and interests of the minorities and Tribals.[61] This committee could be a part of the Constituent Assembly which was to frame the Constitution of India.[62] Attlee's announcement of 20th February 1947 also stated that unless the Constituent Assembly frame a Constitution by June 1947, the British Government would have to consider to whom the powers be handed over.[63] Accordingly the constituent Assembly set up on Advisory Sub-Committee on the North East Tribal and Excluded Areas under the Chairmanship of Assam Premier Gopinath Bordoloi.

Constituent Assembly and Integration of Mizo Hills

By this time, the tribals in north east India were already worried about their political future. The Constituent Assembly which was to frame the future Constitution of India could not ignore the specialised requirements of the excluded and partially excluded areas. To assist the Assembly for the purpose a sub-committee was formed to report on the North East Frontier (Assam) Tribal and Excluded Areas. The sub-committee was to work under the Advisory Committee on Fundamental Rights, Minorities and Tribal and Excluded Areas of which Sardar Patel was the Chairman. The sub-committee was then to have Gopinath

Bordoloi, the Assam Premier as the Chairman. B.N. Rau, the Constitutional Advisor to the Constituent Assembly and a civil service man who had spent several years in Assam was also a member of the committee. The other members were J.J.M. Nichols Roy, the leader of the Khasis, and a Minister in the Bordoloi Cabinet, A.V. Thakkar a Gandhian social worker, Rup Nath Brahmma, a prominent plain tribal intellectual and Mayang Nokcha. The last was subsequently replaced by Aliba Imti Ao, the President of the Naga National Council.[64] The committee which was officially formed in February 27, 1947 extensively toured the province of Assam which included visits to the Lushai hills, North Cachar sub-division, Mikir hills and the Naga hills district.[65] In addition the representatives of the tribes visited the headquarters. The committee received memoranda from various representative and political organisations and also recorded evidence given by prominent citizens and officials. The committee co-opted two members from each of the district it visited.[66]

As far as the Mizos were concerned, both the Mizo Union which was a new political party and the other District Conference, comprising of leading members of the Mizo society claimed to be the representative organisation. The Bordoloi committee accepted Mizo Union as the representative of the Mizo people rather than the Conference stating:

> ... the District Conference convened by the Superintendent of the Lushai hills as an elected body (was) purporting to be representative of the whole of Lushai hills. The election to this body which consisted of twenty chiefs and twenty commoners with the Superintendent himself as President was boycotted by the Mizo Union which was the only representative body of the Lushai at that time and (hence the Conference) could not be regarded by us as representing more than a section of opinion largely that of the officials and chiefs controlled by them.[67]

In fact the District Superintendent wanted that the District Conference be treated as the representative of the Mizo people. The refusal to do so by the Bordoloi Committee and appointing co-opted members from the Mizo Union party infuriated the Superintendent to no end. He complained about it to the Committee that the co-option was done without consulting the District authority.[68]

According to its provision, the sub-committee send invitation to the Mizo Union party to send its nominees to be the co-opted members of the sub-committee. Earlier Bordoloi had invited Vanlawma to be one of the members of the sub-committee. But the situation changed as the Mizo Union had a new set of office bearers now. While the Mizo Union nominated its president Khawtin Khuma and leader Saprawnga to be the members of the sub-committee, Vanlawma urged Khawthinkhuma not to accept the invitation because the Assam Premier had earlier promised the Mizos full membership but now they were being given only co-opted membership. But the Mizo Union accepted the co-opted membership and joined the sub-committee.

Joining the sub-committee had important implications for the Mizos. Since the Constituent Assembly was set up to frame a constitution for free India, participating in it implied consent to be a part of the Indian Union. Due to this even though some Nagas had joined the sub-committee, they later withdrew from it as the Nagas had by then began to contemplate not joining the Indian Union. The Mizos had no representative in the Constituent Assembly but the Bordoloi Committee was an integral part of the Constituent Assembly and its recommendations were going to be incorporated while making the Constitution of India. Hence joining the sub-committee would imply permanent official acceptance to merger. This sparked off a public debate among the Mizo leadership. On the eve of the visit of the Bordoloi subcommittee, a public meeting was organised at Aizawl. Wherein Vanlawma, the former Secretary of Mizo Union and a prominent Mizo leader made an important speech. Vanlawma referred to his meeting with Bordoloi and said when the future of Assam, was in jeopardy, the Assam Premier 'begged' the Mizos to side with Assam so that Assam could join India rather than Pakistan, now that the Cabinet Mission proposals have been rejected and the crisis was over, the Assam Government was even refusing to offer the Mizos full membership in the sub-committee. If this way any indication of the things to come in future. The Mizos should insist on remaining independent.

Unperturbed by these developments, the Committee visited Aizawl, the headquarters of the Lushai hills district on 17th and 18th April, 1947[69] along with two of its Mizo members. During this visit it noted that the people, even though isolated from main stream political life due to the device of 'Excluded Areas' "were not found lacking in political consciousness."[70] "The people of Lushai hills who have benefitted by the activities of the missionaries among them cannot be said to be behind the people of the plains in culture, education and literacy. In literacy particularly they are in a better position than a good number of the plain areas and the general percentage of literacy among them is about 13 percent while among man only is about 30 per cent."[71]

The Commission through the evidence and memoranda also 'noticed' that a school of thought did exist among the Mizos which favoured 'independence'.[72] The Commission suspected this to be the influence of "instigation by certain elements". The Commission also noted the District Conference convened by the district Superintendent had drafted a 'Constitution' by which Mizo hills would manage all its affairs while surrendering only the Defence to the Government of India. A treaty to that effect could be signed with the Government of India.[73] The Committee also appreciated the anxiety expressed by the hill people about their land and exploitation by the advanced sections by the peoples of the Indian plains. Hence they favoured continuation of the devices like the 'Innerline' which were introduced by the colonial authorities and also introduction of new protective laws which would not only ensure the preservation of the life and culture of the tribals but also grant them maximum autonomy.[74]

With the visit of the Committee, the political climate in the Mizo hills was activated again. The factions of the Mizo Union intensified their rivalry. Both the parties submitted separate memoranda to the Commission, the right wing in their memorandum stated that the Mizos differed from the rest of Indians in every way and hence their position would not be secure if they integrated with India. Hence they wanted to be left in the same status as they were prior to the British conquest of the Mizo hills, i.e., independent. Thus the memorandum of the right wing made the 'official' demand of independence for the first time.

According to the schedule prepared by the Superintendent both the rival groups presented themselves before the sub-committee.[75] The right wing was led by Pachunga and Vanlawma while the left wing by Dengthuama and Saprawnga. Even though they could not present any common political demand, the right wing supported the proposals of the District Conference.[76] The left wing was in favour of joining India provided the interests of the tribals were provided constitutional safeguards. But it insisted on the provision for a review of the present arrangement after a period of ten years.[77] The essence of all the evidence presented before the committee was the apprehensions about the plainsman and insecurities of a small community while merging with a massive nation with whom they had very little in common. Hence although they favoured joining the Indian Union, they demanded maximum autonomy to the district to rule themselves and protection of their rights and interest against exploitation by plains people. Even McDonald, the District Superintendent made similar demand in his evidence before the Committee.[78] H. Vanthuama, General Secretary of the Union (left wing) stated that the Lushai hills would be within Indian Union only as long as the Lushai hills was economically backward. As soon as it became economically viable it would part with India. In fact he stated that after ten years the Mizos would secede from India.[79] Pachunga of the right wing wanted the Lushai hills to be directly under the jurisdiction of the Government of India.[80] R. Thanlira, Dengthuama and Bawichuaka pleaded for maximum autonomy. Bawichuaka demanded unification of all the Mizo inhabited areas under one administration and a National Council with independent judiciary, legislative and executive to administer the district. But Bawichuaka insisted on a ten year period following which the Mizos would have the right to self determination.[81] It is to be observed that the members of the Mizo Union (left wing) presented similar view before the committee which were then condensed and systematically presented in the form of a memorandum to the Bordoloi Committee. The Mizo Union had a conference on 22 April 1947 wherein it drafted a memorandum regarding the future of Mizo hills and submitted it to the committee. The memorandum signed by Khawtinkhuma and Vanthuama read, ". . . . At the time when India becomes independent, the Lushai hills district will also be federated with the province of Assam and be connected therewith in certain subjects which shall be desired by negotiations between the provincial legislature and the Mizo National Council. The district will henceforth be called Mizoram including the contiguous areas of Cachar, Chittagong hills tract, Manipur and Tripura. . . . The village with its village council will constitute the unit and basis of administration within Mizoram . . . the financial provision should be made by the centre from year to year until such time as the Mizos shall assert that they are able to maintain their territorial integrity and self-determination without this financial provision . . . all the points suggested by the party shall be subject to revision after ten years."[82]

Mizo Secessionism

The visit of the Bordoloi Committee witnessed the intensification of the separatist movement. This happened because it was felt that joining the Bordoloi committee and expression of the desire to be integrated into the Indian Union by the left wing Mizo Union whom the committee had accepted as the mouthpiece of the Mizos had given it the seal of finality. Now a concerted effort had started in favour of independence. Pachunga, the President of the right wing Mizo Union along with Dahrawka and Hmartawnpunga published a political pamphlet which read:

> We Mizos have nothing in common with the Vai (Indians). If we commit ourselves under the Indian

> government, we Will be swallowed by the Indians because they are much more in number than the Mizo people. Until the British came, we Mizos had nothing to do with the Vai, now that the British are leaving we should get out of the British government to be as we were before, namely, free. The Mizos are neither slaves nor possessions; therefore we should not allow ourselves to be treated as such, having to change owners. The Mizos should stand firm together and defend Mizoram for the Mizo people. Whatever may come Mizoram is for the Mizos.[83]

Earlier than this (May 5, 1947) a pamphlet entitled *Zoram Independent* written by D. Ronghaka was published and distributed in Aizawl. The pamphlet advocated that the Mizos should declare themselves independent. The English translation of the Mizo pamphlet read:

> Every nation in the world strives for independence. India had struggled long to secure its independence. So have the Muslims of India for their independence. If the Mizos do not fight for their independence, they will remain slaves (Tuk Luh Bawi) which practise has been abolished long ago. We should fight for independence to avoid becoming slaves again. The fact that we speak one language (which proves that we are one people) is reason enough for us to strive for independence. Some of us are of the opinion that we should remain within India for the present and seek independence later. But this would prove very difficult. In time there would be some other pharaoh who had power and did not remember our Joseph and if he ordered you to kill your first son you would not be able to disobey it if you are part of India. Our succeeding generations would be in a difficult situation. If we are independent, all of us will be happy because then we will be working for our own future. It might be difficult at the initial period but it would be a worthwhile struggle.
>
> We have heard people say that Mizoram is a rich country. We have deciduous evergreen trees, bamboos, vines and many other plants from which medicines and herbs

can be made. We have plenty of trees bearing fruits. We can increase the number of such trees and sell the fruits to our neighbouring countries. We will also increase our handicraft. We will improve our education. We will have the power to make machines. While the British government ruled us, we could not even make a gun because they provided it to us. We can make anything we want, if we are independent.

Because of our religion alone we should be away from the Indians. All around us, different religious groups seem to form their own countries. The Burmese are Buddhists. The Indians are Hindus and the Pakistanis are Muslims. Why should not we Mizos who are Christians have our own sovereign country. As prophet Isaiah said, "Have faith and it will be done". Let us say, if these people can have separate country, we Mizos can have one too. This is the time for us to take our religion seriously. If Prophet Isaiah had been alive He would have said, Believe in God and start your own government. At the moment some of us are concerned about their own selfish interests. But let us look at the future not just our present. Let us strive to keep this country for our own children and grandchildren, not just think about ourselves.[84]

Following this, a plethora of pamphlets were distributed in Mizoram through which a country-wide debate took place on whether Mizos should remain within India, join Burma, remain under the British or declare themselves independent. Thus the more closer the Indian independence came, the more polarised the Mizo leaders became over the issue of joining India or remaining independent. The pro-India group was led by Vanthuama. The anti-merger group was led by Pachunga who was stripped of his MU position and hence was a dissident. There was also debate over the issue of remaining a part of Assam or be governed by the government of India directly if Mizo hills merged with India. In the midst of all these both the parties seemed to agree with the point raised by Rev. Zairema and R. Thanlira, the editors of *Mizo Daily* that

Mizos should demand as much autonomy as possible even if merger was agreed upon. H.K. Bawichuaka demanded that the Mizos should be given adequate representation in the Assam legislature, widest possible autonomy and amalgamation of all the Mizo inhabited areas into one unit. One of the members of Pachunga faction wanted the Mizos to join the Mizo areas of Burma and form a separate province within Burma.

The MU faction led by Vanlawma and Pachunga continued their campaign for an independent Mizoram. Vanlawma wrote a persuasive piece called *Khawi Lamah Nge I Kal Dawn? Quo vadis* (where are you going).[85] He refuted the argument that the Mizos were 'too stupid' to govern themselves. He provided instances from Bible saying that like the philosophers of Israel who were afraid to leave Egypt were guided by a fire till their destination was reached, Mizos were saved from Japanese invasion. Similarly this time too God would certainly save them from the idol-worshippers (Hindus). Therefore Mizos should not be afraid of seeking independence.

Pachunga too wanted the British not to desert the Mizos till they were able to govern themselves. He sent a Memoranda to the Constituent Assembly, the British Prime Minister Attlee and the opposition leader Churchill to the effect that the British should not leave the Christian Mizos to the mercy of the Hindus.[86] Another similar pamphlet was circulated by K. Zawla which lamented the Mizo's prospective merger with India and advocated Mizo independence.[87]

> It is most beneficial for the Mizos to have the British remain in Mizoram. Instead of having a limited, autonomous district attached to Indian government or Burma government it would be preferable to a limited state attached to the British. Before it is too late, let us consider carefully what is best for us. Imagine the state of things in the near future with Hindi as the official language, because virtually no Mizo spoke Hindi. If you allow the British to leave now, you will greatly regret it later. . . To acquire the desired Mizoram and to make

Mizoram a place in which Jesus could be happy to live, let us ask God for guidance.

When I would go to have a quiet moment alone, not knowing exactly why, I would cry for all the Mizo men in the Mizoram villages because they were forced to carry baggage for the Indian and the British Officials, but now I cried for the Mizos who had formal education, because they wanted to sell Mizoram to the Indian government. As soon as the Mizos joined the Indian government, they would have to pay such taxes as poll tax, land tax, home ownership tax, vehicle tax, bullock tax, car tax and school tax. They will pay more taxes than they ever paid to the British government. In effect, we will be slaves to the Indians.

Therefore, the best thing we can do is to remain under the rule of the British government here in Mizoram. If the British stay in Mizoram for 3 to 5 years and meanwhile we learn from the British how to run our own government, this will be a happy occurrence. If the British remain in Mizoram, our Chiefs will be ruling under some constitutions, and they will not be too much of a burden for the common people; and the Superintendents, knowing the British occupation is limited will not become corrupted by an abundance of power. After 3 to 5 years, if we feel that we want to join either Burma or India, we can join them. We can always be the slave of the Indians.

Let us not hesitate in expressing our desire for the British to extend their stay in Mizoram. We must let the British know how we feel immediately.

Countries such as India, much wealthier than we are, have been granted a degree of autonomy under the British since 1937. To help us set up our own government 3 to 5 years is an obligation which in essence, the British owe us. Remember, when the Superintendent McCall asked the Mizos to declare war against the Japanese, even before the British Indian government declared war officially on Japan, at the beginning of World War-II, he spoke in the name of the King of England and said that after the British won the war, those of us who fought against the Japanese would be granted whatever we asked.

General Slim of the 14th British Army said, 'The Lushai have clearly shown your friendship to the British. When the British lacked man and ammunition, and the Japanese seemed unbeatable, our summer friends deserted us. Contrary to our summer friends, the Lushai carried on their traditions of honesty and bravery: their British officers and their Chiefs determined to defend their country and worked hard to do so. And when the enemy arrived at the India-Burma border, the Lushai Scouts were in the front lines, and stopped the Japanese. Mizo bravery and honesty will never be forgotten by us. In my opinion, those Mizo Scouts should be awarded a new status that of Soldier of the Empire.'

Look at the good words said about us in the above quotation. General Slim will obviously cooperate with us in whatever area we desire. Let us not get involved unnecessarily in the turbulent politics outside of Mizoram. Let us believe and have faith in God. If Mizos want to be parasites, why not continue to be parasitic to the British. . . .

Question: We Mizos are rather insignificant. Would the British be willing to help us?

Answer: We don't need to worry about that now. The British are obligated to teach the Indians for 11 years. The British are obligated to help us learn to govern ourselves.

Although it may seem not practicable for the British to help us in this matter, remember that the British have many colonies, we are not the least of them.

Question: Will the Indian government release us now that we are already apart from it?

Answer: Let us stop worrying about what the Indians will do; remember the Indians just want us as their slaves. Mizoram is not really a part of India; it is actually an "excluded area." If you want to appeal you case beyond the Superintendent, you have to appeal to the Governor, not to the Assam Legislature. The British government includes Mizoram under British India. The aid we have received from the British government is not from the Assam Legislature, but from the British Assam Governor. While the Hindus and Muslims were rulers in India, we never were a part of them. Therefore, we have a good opportunity to choose our own future today.

Question: Will it not be an embarrassment to the British, now that they have stated their intention to leave India, to remain indefinitely in Mizoram?

Answer: The British government is giving cooperation with its former colonies in granting conditions under which independence is come about. This is why Pakistan exists today. Some countries now feel that freedom means any states in which the British are gone, but if we define freedom for ourselves as involving the temporary continuing presence of the British, that is our right.

For those people in the "excluded area", which included Mizoram, the British have appointed an Advisory Committee. This Advisory Committee will see that the wishes of the tribal peoples in "excluded areas" are carried out, especially since many tribal representatives have been appointed to the Committee. If we demand what we desire to, the Indian, rather than the British will be embarrassed by the British presence in Mizoram.

Question: The fact the Mizoram has no outlet to the ocean, will India or Pakistan allow the British to pass through their territories in order to get to Mizoram?

Answer: I am certain that India and Pakistan will allow the British free passage. If they offended the

> British, they will find it difficult to trade with any country in the world since the British controlled most of the world's seas. . .
>
> As I said, it is most beneficial to the Mizos to have the British remain in Mizoram. Instead of having a limited autonomy, attached to the Indian government or the Burma government, it would be preferable to have a limited autonomous state attached to the British. Before it is too late, let us consider carefully what is best for us. Imagine the state of things in the near future with Hindi as the official language, virtually no Mizos spoke Hindi. If you allow the British to leave now, you will greatly regret it later. I am eager to know how many of you agree with me. To acquire the desired Mizoram and to make Mizoram a place in which Jesus could be happy to live, let us ask God for guidance.[88]

As a culmination of this process on July 5, 1947, another party known as the United Mizo Freedom Organisation surfaced under the leadership of Lalbiakthanga an ex-Burmese Mizo military officer from Burma. Lalbiakthanga, assumed presidentship of the organisation while Hmingliana and L.H. Liana were Vice President and General Secretary respectively. Lalbiakthanga believed that it would be difficult to talk of an Independent Mizoram after 15th August 1947. Therefore complete independence and the unification of all the contiguous Mizo areas should be sought now before the boundaries between India, Pakistan and Burma were demarcated. Given a choice UMFO did not mind joining Burma too. The party received a boost, when all members of the Pachunga group of the MU, except Vanlawma joined the UMFO.[89]

Apart from the right wingers, the party was supported by the rich and chiefs' council.[90] Its seccessionist character and objective as was evident from the name itself, earned it the support of the chiefs and rich businessmen who provided it with financial assistance. The chiefs' Council selected Lalmawia, the founder leader of the Lushai Students' Association and an ex-army officer in Burma to work out a modified plan to keep Mizoram out of India and also mobilise public opinion in favour of it.[91] (Lalmawia later became the President of the party when Lalbiakthanga left the party.) But when the party prepared its constitution it did not make its seccessionist character very explicit. This was done to depict that this party's aim was not different from the (left wing) Mizo Union Party which was already immensely popular among the masses.[92] The constitution listed the objectives of the party as:

1. To look for a country with which we could identify ourselves and which we admit and which can provide us the benefits.
2. To promote true democratic spirits where people can choose their own leaders and to reject all traces of authoritarianism.
3. To make our country as strong as possible so that it need not depend on other countries.
4. To improve our culture
5. To try to better our communication and understanding between ruler and the ruled.
6. To develop the best ways of self administration.
7. To ensure freedom of speech and press.
8. To ensure freedom of religion.[93]

Lalmawia who served in Burma had contacts with the tribal chiefs of Burma. It is said that on the instructions of the Chiefs' Council, he discussed the feasibility of forming a Union of the Hill areas of Burma and the Lushai hills with the tribal chiefs of Falam — Zahrelian. Lalmawia and the chief agreed to unite. But the Burmese Government did not encourage the idea of merging Mizoram with Burma as it had already opted for India.[94] This fizzled out the UMFO movement for merger with Burma and with it the UMFO party because by then India had become independent.

One of the most important contribution of the UMFO was to officially start a movement for joining Burma. For sometime the movement caught the fancy of certain sections of the Mizo people. The arguments advanced in favour of merger with Burma was, Mizos were ethnically very close to the Burmese and their languages were very similar. Economically, along with Burma, the Mizos could enter the international market for its bamboo and other goods. Politically it would be more advantageous to join Burma as it was smaller than India and hence Burma would grant the Mizos a voice in the political affairs.[95]

However, there was very little time for the UMFO to become popular or mobilise public opinion in support of its programmes. But it could not make any inroads into the Mizo Union stronghold. The base of the Union were the masses. The masses refused to receive the ideas of UMFO. The people wanted to be rid of the chiefs whereas the UMFO was the party of the chiefs. In fact the party was known as the *Zalen Pawl*[96] or the 'party of the priviledged'. Hence they rejected the UMFO and without the support of the common people the UMFO simply faded out.

In view of the increasing momentum of the secessionist movement the Mizo Union seemed to be losing out. To gain losing ground they prepared to send its volunteers to the villages and interior areas to campaign for the merger of Mizoram with India and popularise the issue of Indian independence. Vankhama and Lalrinliana were sent to Sialsuk (east of Aizawl); Vanlalliana (son of Pachunga) and Challeta were sent to Champai (east of Aizawl), Ngura and his friends to the north east and Thangridema and Thantuma were sent to Baktawng.[97] These volunteers, during their extensive tour in the interior of Mizo hills, to accomplish their mission, however discovered that the common people had no idea of the impending British withdrawal. Reeling under the oppression of the chiefs these villagers did not care about the future of Mizoram whether it joined India, Burma or emerges independent. What they desired was riddance of the chiefs. A folk song of the Mizos of that period reflected their desire,

bai thak arva
artui khawn leh
lal hnungzui reng ka ning tawh
kawltu chawi lai daltu an ni
sazai lian pui an ni

(We are fed up of submitting to the chief's orders. He wants us to do all his work. He demands eggs and chickens. We have to always carry out his orders and in the process get delayed for our own work. This is indeed a severe punishment).

Another similar song read:

zalen muhil lo tho r'u
ni a chhuak sang tawh em e
in kawmawl ahho reng hi
a lum lua e ka ti

The Mizo volunteers reported this to the party from which the MU think-tank picked up the thread. It referred to the Congress's promise to abolish monarchy and Zamindari system and obtained a promise from the Bordoloi government that after the British withdrawal, chieftainship would be abolished which was popularised among the masses. This created a sensational turn in Mizo politics. Enthused by the promise, people rallied round the MU. They called the UMFO *as rorel khawl* meaning party of the privileged. The Mizo Union organised a crusade against the chiefs and even launched a civil disobedience against the chiefs. The tempo rose. There was confrontation between the chiefs and the commoners. Alarmed at the prospect the chiefs began to support the UMFO which weakened the Mizo independence movement and strengthened the merger movement. This was also recorded in a classical Mizo folk song:

India zawm duh chu lal banna
independence duh chu lal lalna

which means joining India would ensure the abolition of chieftainship, but independence means its continuation.

and,

union le union a dang mange
union vantlang kan tanrual laiin
dawrpuii union ve che rual elna

(Though both the parties are called Mizo Union, they are different from each other. While the Mizo Union is trying to unite the people, the Dawrpuii (Pachunga) faction speaks ill of others and cause disunity.)

In the meantime McDonald was replaced by Penn for a very short time who was in turn replaced by L.L. Peters as the District Superintendent. The extensive support for merger sidelined the UMFO and strengthened MU. Enthused by this Khawtinkhuma of MU prepared for a procession in Aizawl to celebrate India's independence on 15th August 1947. The Pachunga-Vanlanwa faction tried to prevent the procession and wrote to Khawtinkhuna to that effect.[98] If done so a violent confrontation might break out. It also asked the District Superintendent not to hoist the Indian flag in Mizoram on that day.

On 14th night a MU meeting took place in Dawrpui Veng. When the situation became very tense the procession was postponed. The Superintendent called a meeting on the same day, in which about fifty Mizos attended and a resolution was passed which read:[99]

1. Resolved that owing to the unexpected acceleration of the date of transfer of power by the British government and as the Lushai's have not yet been definitely informed in detail as to what is the proposed future constitution and form of administration of the district and as section (7) sub-section (2) of Indian Independence Bill does not clarify the situation, it is accordingly thought necessary that his Excellency the Governor of Assam should kindly inform them in writing as to what these are to be, also whether the Lushais are at this stage allowed the option of joining any other Dominion i.e. Pakistan or Burma.

Resolved further that the Superintendent Lushai hills should communicate the above request of the Lushais to the advisor to His Excellency the Governor of Assam in order to clarify these points.

2. Resolved if the Lushais are to enter Indian Union their main demands are:

a) that the existing safeguards of customary laws and land tenure etc. should be maintained.
b) that the Chin hills Regulation 1896 and Bengal Eastern Frontier Regulation 1873 should be retained until such times as the Lushais themselves through parallel district authority declare that these can be abrogated.

3. That the Lushais will be allowed to opt out of the Indian Union when they wish to do so subject to a minimum period of ten years.

The meeting was attended by both the MU factions but the pro-Independence faction however was in a minority. However on 15th August there was no untoward incident when Mizo hills formally became a part of India. The resolution was the final acceptance of the inclusion of Mizoram in the Indian Union signed by the accredited leaders of the Mizo people. The integration of the Mizo hills with the Indian Union, was thus given legitimacy.

Merger of Manipur

The British paramountcy came to an end on 15th August 1947. Ripples of India's celebration reached the shores of Manipur too. The Indian tri-colour fluttered everywhere — roads, maidan, market and villages. Resounding voices of Bande Mataram was heard far and wide: "There was none including women and children who did not feel their hearts with happy abandon on this particular day."[100] The Maharaja of Manipur gained full control of administration once again after 86 years. But at this juncture Manipur was at a very critical point of her history. On the one hand it witnessed a massive movement for responsible government and on the other there were preparations underway among the Congressites to effect its merger with Indian Union. The then Dominion Agent, Debeshwar Sharma, was pressing the Centre for integration of Manipur as a district of Assam, there was even a suggestion that Manipur should be merged with West Bengal.[101] In mid-September Sardar Patel mooted a scheme for the formation of Purbanchal Pradesh consisting of Manipur, Cachar, Lushai hills and Tripura.[102] Irabat found the whole idea of Purbanchal Pradesh 'nauseatic'.[103] He felt this would be a threat to the distinctive social, cultural, political and historical identity of Manipur. He therefore strongly opposed the idea and implored people to fight tooth and nail against it.

The dilly-dallying tactics of the Maharaja in granting a responsible government generated public hostility against him. On 4th October 1947 the Congress Working Committee passed a resolution for 'immediately granting Responsible government,'—the deadline to which was given as 1st April 1948.[104] The Maharaja assured the people of adult franchise, elected legislature and a ministry of elected representatives. But the political leaders could not rely upon his word and started agitation. Demonstrations and picketing in front of state offices, at the residence of the government officials, were resorted to. This non-stop agitation completely paralyzed the function of the government and normal life in Manipur.[105] On 10th November the Government gave threats of retaliation and stoppage of 'war compensation.'[106] But the movement was more intensified. This development compelled the Chief Minister of the Interim Council to make a declaration on 23rd November that a Responsible Government would be introduced within six months. The election was held on 11 June 1948 under the supervision of Franchise Sub-Committee.[107] No party could secure an absolute majority in the election though Congress emerged as the largest majority. Consequently a non-Congress coalition government was formed and Maharaja Kumar Priyabrata Singh became the first Chief Minister. The maiden session of the Assembly was called on 18th October, 1948.[108]

The election result gave a jolt to the aspirations of the Congressites. It also sealed the fate of the idea of Purbanchal Pradesh. The local Congress unit established closer links with the area. It invited Prafull Chandra Ghose an eminent Congressman from Bengal who in his speech favoured the idea of Purbanchal Pradesh. But peoples' opposition to the idea made the situation tense.[109] At a public meeting held on 18th September all the leaders of both the hills and plains strongly opposed the move and declared that the people of Manipur would resist any type of imposition of the proposed province. The government of Manipur also opposed the idea.[110] Due to such strong opposition the proposal of the Manipur State Congress for the creation of Purbanchal Pradesh was nipped in the bud.

Irabat Singh who contested on the Krishak Sabha ticket and was returned from Utlou constituency, not only opposed the Purbanchal Pradesh idea, he demanded the restoration of Kabaw Valley which was transferred to Burma from Manipur. The workers of his Krishak Sabha and Praja Sangha started mobilising the villagers and organised several meetings in villages. Irabat was a confirmed Communist by now and his activities roused suspicion in the Government circles.[111] Sir Akbar Hydari the Governor of Assam, visited Manipur to study the situation. The political activities of Irabat specially was minutely observed and studied. This had become essential in view of the increasing rumour of a communist coup in Manipur and Irawat's opposition to the merger of Manipur with India.[112] It was reported that the higher level of the Indian government felt that if Irabat was allowed to move freely it would be impossible to effect the merger. Irabat was also held responsible for all the disturbances in Manipur. The Manipur government in a move to curb his activities banned the Krishak Sabha, Praja Sangh, Mahila Sammilla and Student Federation — the organisations Irawat was associated with.[113]

Irabat on the other hand founded the state unit of the Communist Party of India after the second Congress of the CPI was held in Calcutta (28 February — 6 March 1948).[114] This was the time when peasants were engaged in armed struggle in Telengana, Bengal and Tripura. Irabat's day as a free moving citizen came to an end on 21st September 1948. On this day as he was tried to be arrested thus compelling him to go underground. Irabat started popularising communist ideology and programmes from underground. He also started mobilising and organising the peasants.

Irabat was trying to start a Telengana-like uprising in Manipur and establish an 'Independent Peasant Republic of Manipur'.[115] In fact one of the reasons that the Home Ministry of India hastened the process of merger of Manipur with India was the rising spectre of communist armed struggle in various parts of India which had given rise to this phenomenon called 'Communist Menace'.[116]

The Indian National Congress favoured the inclusion of all the former Princely States into the fold of the Dominion of India. At its session of 15th June 1947, the Congress Party adopted a resolution which declared that "they could not admit the right of any state in India to declare its independence and to live in isolation from the rest of India."[117] This process of integration was to be achieved before India was declared a 'Republic.' As far as Manipur was concerned, the Indian Government desired to settle the merger issue by means of 'conciliation and pressure'.[118] As a first step they asked the Maharaja to sign the 'Stand-Still Agreement'.[119] The Maharaja desired to establish a close relationship between Manipur and the Dominion of India and hence he agreed to the conditions of the Stand-Still Agreement and signed it on 11 August 1947.[120] According to it the government of Manipur accepted to entrust the responsibilities of defence, communication and external affairs to the care of the Indian government. Apart from this other ancillary subjects like custom, excise and coinage etc. were also surrendered to the government of India. The internal administration was the sole authority of the Maharaja and the Government of India assured the protection of internal autonomy and authority of Manipur. But unfortunately it had not specified the future political status of Manipur.

After the independence of India the office of Dominion Agent was established who was to be the Indian resident representative in Manipur. Debeshwar Sharma was appointed for the post. The nature of post was such that it gave immense opportunity and power to the agent to interfere in the state politics and take sides. Sir Akbar Hydari's report on Sharma, after his visit of Manipur brought not only the dismissal of Sharma but also abolition of the post of Agent and in his place a 'Dewan' was appointed. Akbar Hydari's sudden death brought Sri Prakash as the Governor of Assam. Sri Prakash's visit of Manipur created panic in Manipur as it was rumoured that he was there to effect merger.[121] Sri Prakash, sensing this, declared that he had no intention of destroying the political identity of Manipur.[122] But his actions proved otherwise. There were intelligence report about the preparations for a communist coup in Manipur. The state Superintendent of Police, S. Palit covered a vast area to confirm that some workers of the Communist Party of Manipur were actually trying to collect arms and ammunitions and had launched a propaganda campaign in the Nungbung Awangba area, some 20 miles east of Imphal to win the Naga tribals in their favour.[123] Strict vigil and army was maintained in Nambol — The constituency of the Communist leader Irabat which was viewed as the potential centre where from the uprising could start. The unconstitutional appointment of Major Rawal Aman Singh as the 'Dewan' of Manipur by the Governor was a move to counter the Communist insurgency. In a confidential letter to the Advisor to the Governor of Assam, Nari Rustomji, Major Singh stated that he was doing all he could to put a check on the activities of the Communists in the state, but there was collaboration between the Manipuri and Burmese Communists and he would not be surprised if there was some kind of a flare up.[124]

The function of the 'Dewan' in Manipur was general supervision and guidance in the matters relating to administration of Manipur. The Dewan was also to hold the direct charges of (1) law and order; (2) administration of Hill areas and relations with the Government of India. Thus the Dewan was made the virtual overall In-charge of Manipur's administration which annoyed the helpless Maharaja. Major General Rawal Amar Singh was appointed the Dewan with Major Khating as his deputy.[125] By the middle of 1949, the Government of India had apparently decided to integrate Manipur within the Indian Union. The intention of the Indian Government to accede Manipur into India was becoming manifestly clear. Even the secret conferences between the State Congress unit and the AICC had become an open secret.[126] The Praja Shanti Sabha a strong political party took strong exception to the negotiations and opposed the impending merger.[127] In a meeting (25th August 1949) it pleaded to the Government of India to maintain the status quo and allow the separate identity of Manipur outside India. But, the writings of the wall were clear. On 8th September 1949 a public meeting was organised by the Youth Socialist League where except the State Congress every party spoke against the merger and asked the Maharaja not to sign any document in favour of the integration.

Soon after the Manipur State Congress got blessings direct from New Delhi, they called a public meeting at Imphal on the 3rd August, 1949, in which they promised that they would convey to the people the assurances they received from the Indian leaders. The people expected to hear assurances against the possible merger. (The Congress workers had taken photographs of the assembled crowd to be sent to New Delhi as proof of mass support to the Manipur State Congress). But they found that the assurances were for merger of Manipur into the Centre, and that the meeting itself was not a 'public meeting' but of Congress workers. They immediately held another public meeting at the Gandhi Maidan, Imphal, on the same day under the joint presidentship of Solet Haokip Kuki, Habi Dewan Mahamed and Nandalal Sharma. The following were the resolutions adopted in the meeting:

1. The big gathering of today's protest public meeting unanimously pass the resolution that the *gaddi* cannot be abolished and the State cannot be integrated or merged.
2. This meeting unanimously resolves that the Manipur State Congress is a deceitful one.
3. This meeting condemns the Manipur State Congress in their act of selling the Manipur prajas to India without taking public opinion and by falsely alleging that they had the support of the people. This meeting further expresses its utter denial of the deceitful plan for a public meeting on their return from Delhi. The Praja

> Santi Sabha be requested to perform the function of informing the Manipuri public and all authorities concerned clearly explaining all these faults and cheatings of the Manipur State Congress.[128]

On the 15th August, 1949, the Manipur State Congress had celebrated the Independence Day at Imphal peacefully. Some 4,000 people took part in the meeting and there were processions with National Flags and music etc. Krishnamohan Singh had presided over the meeting and they shouted *Bande Mataram, Shadhin Bharati Ki Jai, Down with Maharaja and Down with Gaddi*. The Manipur Student's Federation had also observed *Dibashpalan Day* by hoisting black flags at Iril Khongnangkhong (Porompat). Only 200 people had attended the function and they passed a resolution condemning the Congress Government. N. Binoy Singh, son of Dr. Leiren who had been the P.W.D. Minister, hoisted the black flag. The event of this flag hoisting ceremony came out in detail in the *Praja Tantra* paper of 17th August, 1949, under the caption "Shameful News":

> On the 15th August, 1949, the Manipur Student's Federation held a protest meeting by hoisting a Black Flag at Porompat. Cyclostyled bulletins were also distributed. Last year, Dr. Leiren Singh, the present Minister-in-charge of Education held a procession by hoisting a black flag on the 15th August, 1948, at Khurai (Lamlong). By that time this gentleman had not been selected a Minister. This year Srijut N. Binoy Singh, who is the son of this gentleman has performed the function on behalf of the Manipur Student's Federation.[129]

Immediately the Manipur State Police along with the help of a platoon of the Manipur Rifles had started house searchings for all the members who were suspected to belong either to the Communist Party of Manipur or the Manipur Student's Federation. On 22nd August, 1949, houses of the active workers were searched and Communist literatures of leaflets were seized.

All members of the party in the Legislative Assembly adopted a resolution to oppose the merger. It read:

> "If integration or merging be imposed here irrespective of our unfortunate helpless circumstances and (violating) the principle of Bapuji, without the consent of the people, the present moral submission of the Manipuris to India, which is most precious, may disappear bidding good-bye to the physical control of imposition and the bitter experiences thereof may be a short of handicap in the political races of India with other countries a double loss for India and Manipur. If the people have been sinned against and wronged, the people themselves have to be watched over in addition to the watch over across the frontier."[130]

As against this the Manipur State Congress adopted a resolution favouring strongly the merger.[131] They even decided to send a delegation of three members of the party to meet AICC leaders in New Delhi to expedite and facilitate the merger. In fact the merger was necessary in view of the:

1. Incapability of the government of Manipur to maintain law and order situation in the country;
2. The apprehensions from the activities of the communist revolution in Burma; and
3. The merger would ensure peace and development in Manipur.[132]

The Maharaja was not unaware of the developments and the impending crisis. But he was held and was being virtually dictated by the Diwan. In the meantime the relationship between the Dewan and the Maharaja deteriorated on account of the Dewan's constant interference in internal administration. Annoyed with the interference the Maharaja left for Shillong, capital of Assam on 15th September 1949 and reached there on 17th. The Governor replied the it would be a pleasure to receive[133] the Maharaja and offer him hospitality. The Governor seized this unexpected opportunity and laid the trap. He had already been briefed by the 'Diwan' that the Maharaja was in the hands of unscrupulous individuals which because a plea for him not to negotiable with any other individual or bodies except the Maharaja himself. When the Maharaja reached the Government House at Shillong, he was completely upset to see unexpected arrangements. He was informed by the Governor that the Government of India had instructed him to complete the negotiations with the Maharaja regarding the merger before 20th September 1949.[134] The Maharaja wrote a letter to the Governor on 18th that he wanted to talk to the representatives of the people in the Manipur Assembly.

> "Now that the sovereignty of the state has been vested in the people, it would be in the fitness of things to hear the people's voice and learn their sentiments so that the line of action may not in any case be unconstitutional."[135]

After his first meeting with Sri Prakasa, the Governor of Assam in the forenoon of 18th September, Maharaja Bodh Chandra initially thought that he could perhaps slip away from Shillong and thereby evade a final decision on the Governor's unpleasant proposition about the integration of Manipur. He could not yet imagine himself to be a prisoner in the hands of Sri Prakasa and his Advisor, N.K. Rustomji. Because on the 18th September itself, the Relands, which was the Maharaja's residence in Shillong, was encircled by armed security personnel, and the plain clothes checked and followed everybody going in and out of the building. The Maharaja and his party were absolutely cut off from the outside world. Not a single letter and not even a telegram from Manipur (except one in Manipuri about Sri Govindajee's puja) had reached them, nor any information could leak out from there, though many letters and telegrams were despatched from either side. In addition, the Redlands had no telephone connection. The Maharaja's body guards of eight riflemen from the Manipur Rifles were also nothing more than ornamental, as the number of forces surrounding them were significantly increased in the subsequent days. Sri Prakasa could not pay more attention to the Maharaja's appeal to withdraw the armed forces from his own residential quarters. The officiating Private Secretary to His Highness the Maharaja of Manipur therefore ventured to inform the Superintendent of Police, Shillong, in the following manner:

> I am directed to convey the grateful thanks of His Highness the Maharaja of Manipur for your sending guards for the protection of His Highness during his stay here in Shillong. Indeed, His Highness feels glad at the gestures.
>
> But since His Highness has brought adequate guards for himself, His Highness does not like to cause any trouble to you. Hence you can please arrange to withdraw your guards forthwith.[136]

In the same evening of the 18th September, 1949, Sri Prakasa had informed Maharaja Bodh Chandra to come to Government House the next day (19th September) at 9.30 in the morning in order to complete the discussion of the 18th morning. The Governor further stated that he had been given definite instructions by the Hon'ble Minister of States to complete the 'negotiations' by the 20th September, 1949 positively. Maharaja Bodh Chandra was not unaware of the facts that the subject matter had certainly involved the fate of future Manipur. He could not deny his receipt of a number of representatives and resolutions from the people of Manipur concerning 'this very important affair'.

Although Maharaja Bodh Chandra had shown a little resistance out of courtesy to the Governor's proposition, he was personally satisfied to learn from the Governor's Adviser that if the administration of the Manipur State had to be taken over by the Central Government at New Delhi, he would be entitled to a sum of rupees two lakhs and twenty-five thousand per year as his privy purse for life-time. Maharaja Bodh Chandra had shamelessly requested the Governor to move the India Government to raise the amount to the extent of rupees four lakhs.[137]

In the early morning of the 19th September, 1949, Maharaja Bodh Chandra expressed his desire to leave Shillong for Imphal in the afternoon of the same day, since no reply came from the Governor to the contrary. He even informed Sri Prakasa that all the papers connected with the discussions of the 18th September, could be returned to Imphal. He wrote to the Maharaja to come at once in order to finalise the matter. Sri Prakasa had already communicated to Delhi to the States Ministry on the late night of the 18th September all that had transpired at their meeting of the 18th morning, and he received back very "strict instructions" that the negotiations would have to be completed before Maharaja Bodh Chandra left Shillong. Sri Prakash telegraphed Sardar Patel saying that the Maharaja "threatened to return to Manipur without holding any discussions" and he "must not under any circumstances be allowed to return to Manipur."[138] Sri Prakasa sought authority to detain the Maharaja if need be. The Sardar simply enquired "whether he had not a Brigadier in Shillong."[139] The Maharaja knew very well that if he was compelled to work independently of his people, his actions would become very unjustifiable. Therefore, he requested the Governor to allow him to go back to Imphal and thus bring a very speedy solution of the matter. But Sri Prakasa said that he was under the strictest orders of the Government of India to have the negotiations completed without any further delay. He cunningly referred to one of Maharaja Bodh Chandra's letters (Secret Memo of 11th August, 1949) wherein His Highness had requested the Governor to grant an interview in Shillong regarding the affairs of the Manipur State. It was, Sri Prakasa said, in compliance of the Maharaja's request that the meeting had been arranged:

> I have had the opportunity, since, to have discussions with the Hon'ble Minister of States, and have, therefore, no alternative but to communicate the decision of the Government of India to Your Highness and negotiate the final settlement of Your Highness's Privy Purse on the lines of the instructions that have been given to me.[140]

As the Governor had already indicated in his letter of 19th September, Maharaja Bodh Chandra went to meet Sri Prakasa in between 9 and 10 A.M. of 20th September at the Government House. There they had discussed on the subject of the "greatest delicacy", and in the meeting the Maharaja was again assured by Sri Prakasa that the Government of India would certainly protect the ultimate interest of the Maharaja. Sri Prakasa further told the Maharaja that he would be coming personally at the Redlands at 5 P.M. of the same day (20th September). But before the Governor came at the Redlands, Maharaja Bodh Chandra wrote a very strange note to Sri Prakasa wherein there came out a tune of a sudden change in his attitude. The following letter clearly indicated that the Maharaja's will had snapped somewhere:

> Like all other patriots of India I too am a great lover of the Indians for whose welfare I am always anxious. The Manipuris are also Indians. I therefore, always have the good wishes of the people and India at heart. It is also in the best interest of India that the will of the people ought to be taken into consideration.
>
> I consider that I have a guardian in the person of Your Excellency who guides and helps me in my endeavour towards ameliorating the welfare of my people. The only thing is that this being a great change it should be done constitutionally and democratically with an eye to the will of the people whose co-operation I confidently hope we will secure.[141]

As was pre-arranged, Sri Prakasa and his Adviser N.K. Rustomji came to meet the Maharaja exactly at 5 P.M. and had their secret discussions. In the late evening Sri Prakasa wrote another letter to Maharaja Bodh Chandra stating that he was glad indeed since they were able to arrive at happy conclusions during their discussions. After formal courtesies Sri Prakasa again invited the Maharaja *to come in the morning of 21st September at 9* A.M. But Maharaja Bodh Chandra said he would not be able to come in the morning owing to the strain caused in the last night, and so half-past two in the afternoon would be convenient for him. In the meanwhile Sri Prakasa got the *Merger Agreement* typed incorporating all the additions and amendments made therein in accordance with the Maharaja's wishes. In the last meeting with Sri Prakasa at 2.30 in the afternoon, Maharaja Bodh Chandra had put his royal signature on the *Merger Agreement.*

The Merger Agreement was signed on 21st September 1949 but under strictures from the Home Ministry it was officially announced on the 15th October 1949 when the Maharaja was back to Imphal. With that Manipur ceased to be an independent monarchy and became a part of Indian Union as a part 'C' State. It is interesting to note that Sri Prakash did not want the Maharaja to consult the legally constituted State Assembly or the Manipur State Council. It refused to recognise this duly elected bodies. Instead the Government of India stated:

> "The Government of India have throughout dealt with your highness directly as the Ruler of the State and are not prepared to make any deviation at the present stage from the procedure hitherto followed. Your highness may rest assured that the Government of India will take complete responsibility in matter of meeting whatever objection may be raised by the people of the State."[142]

Although Maharaja Bodh Chandra had signed the *Merger Agreement* on the 21st September, people in Manipur remained ignorant and completely unaware of the drastic happenings in Shillong. In the Editorial column of the *Bhagyavati Patrika*, dated 20th September, 1949, an article appeared reflecting the peoples' desire against the merger policy of the Indian Government:

> There must be kinship, and we should not forget that Manipuri nation will surely wither away from the day it is abolished. Anarchy will then be the order of the day; people will lose moorings and not understand the very purpose of life.
>
> We are insulting the honour of our forefathers if the consequence of an Independent India is going to be the enslavement of Manipur through dethronement of the Meitei King. Not a single patriot, not a single nationalist would support or agree to the abolition of the *gaddi*. We urge upon His Highness Maharaja Bodh Chandra

> Singh not to surrender the dignity and honour of the Manipuri nation. Kinship in Manipur must be protected.[143]

Another Editorial article of the *Bhagyavati Patrika* of 21st September, 1949, appeared in a somewhat prejudicial tone which of course incited the people of Manipur to take recourse to murder and blood-shed if the State was integrated to the Centre. The article was printed as follows:

> About 50 years ago, a British Chief Commissioner came to Manipur and he was killed here. There is again a rumour about another Chief Commissioner, and the people are reminded of the Chief Commissioner who lost his life. They ought to remember the incident, for it is now a critical point in Manipur's history. If an Indian Chief Commissioner arrives here, it might be the case of History repeats itself, and, we are afraid, Manipur may witness a mini-scale war.[144]

NOTES

1. R. Suntharalingam, *Indian Nationalism: A Historical Analysis*, (Vikas, New Delhi), p. 459.
2. Ibid, also V.P. Menon, *The Story of the Integration of the Indian States*, (Calcutta, 1961 reprint).
3. Ibid.
4. Ibid.
5. Ibid., Sumit Sarkar, *Modern India* (MacMillan, New Delhi, 1983), p. 449.
6. Ibid., R.J. Moore, *Endgames of the Empire: Studies of Britain's Indian Problem*, (OUP, 1988), p. 189.
7. R. Suntharalingam, op. cit., p. 460
8. Ibid.
9. Ibid.
10. Sumit Sarkar, op. cit., p. 451.
11. R.J. Moore, op. cit., pp. 174–201.
12. *Ibid.*
13. Ibid.
14. Sumit Sarkar, op. cit., p. 441
15. E.M.S. Namboodiripad, *National Question in Kerala*, Bombay, 1952.
16. Ibid., also Sumit Sarkar, op. cit.
17. Sumit Sarkar, op. cit., p. 443
18. Ibid.

19. Ibid., p. 450
20. V.P. Menon, op. cit, p. 46, cited in ibid.
21. Sarkar, ibid.
22. Ibid., p. 450.
23. Ibid., p. 451.
24. Ibid., p. 413.
25. Ibid., p. 446.
26. N. Sanjaoba, 'The Genesis of Insurgency' in Sanjaoba (ed.) *Manipur: Past and Present* (Delhi, 1990). pp. 245–290.
    In his letter to Patel, 26 May 1948, Bordoloi wrote, ". . . It has therefore been absolutely necessary that these trends towards separatist (communist) uprising shall be observed from day to day and the Dominion Government and the Government of Assam should be kept appraised of them. . . while therefore I am completely agreeable to allow autonomy to the State of Manipur, I would not like the State Government to feel that all it should do is to satisfy the Governor of Assam personally and should have no other consideration for their conduct." cited ibid,
27. As can be seen below.
28. Pethic Lawrence to Mountbatten, 12 April 1947, letter no. 134, and N. Mansergh (ed.), *Transfer of Power*, 1942–47, Vol. X, (London, 1981).
29. Mountbatten to Earl of Listowel, 24 April 1947, letter no. 210, in *Ibid.*
30. Andrew Clow, Public Address in Mokukchung, February 1947.
31. Charles Pawsey, DC, Naga Hills District, Address to the Nagas, cited in ibid, pp. 170–171.
32. Asoso Yunou, *The Rising Nagas: A Historical and Political Study*, (Delhi, 1974), pp. 170–71.
33. NNC Memorandum to G.N. Bordoloi, Chairman, Sub-Committee on the Future Administration of the Tribal and Excluded Areas, Kohima, 27 May, 1947.
34. As in note–32.
35. T. Sakhrie, Welcome Address to Akbar Hydari, 26 June, 1947.
36. Asoso Yunou, op. cit., pp. 172–79.
37. T. Aliba, Imti, *Reminiscences: Impur to Naga National Council* (Mokokchung, 1988), pp. 66–68.
38. Ibid.
39. Asoso Yunou, op. cit., p. 175.
40. Ibid.
41. T. Aliba, Imti, op. cit., p. 68.
42. Ibid.
43. A. Yunou, op. cit., p. 200.
44. Ibid., p. 175
45. M. Zinyo, *Phizo and the Naga Problem*, (Dimapur, 1979), p. 20.
46. A. Yunou, op. cit., pp. 200–201.
47. Ibid.
48. T. Aliba, Imti, op. cit., p. 69. Aliba gives the date of the meeting as 23rd July in his Memoir which cannot be correct as it preceeded their meeting with Gandhi which took place on 19th July.

49. Ibid.
50. This was corroborated in the Government of India, *Collected Works of Mahatma Gandhi*, LXXXVIII, May 25, 1947 to July 31, 1947 (New Delhi, 1983), p. 373. Which was based on the 'record of Pyarelal'. Gandhi mentioned about this meeting in his letter to Rammanohar Lohia on June 22, 1947. See ibid. p. 395. But the literal version given above is different from the one published by the Naga leaders although in essence it was similar to each other. Gandhi told them that if they don't even produce their own clothes they were slaves of foreigners. Even though no one could deprive them of their independence, they could not live in complete isolation. Gone are the days when one nation could use army to snatch freedom of others and as far as India was concerned the Nagas were safe.
51. Ibid.
52. Ibid.
53. Phizo to the President of India, 1-11-1957, cited in Ibid. Also Girija Kumar V.K. Arora (ed.), *Documents on Indian Affairs*, New Delhi, 1965, p. 108.
54. In fact if anybody can be hailed as the father of Naga Nation it was T. Aliba Imti who was the maker of Naga National Council. Similarly T. Sakharie was one of the former leaders of the NNC and had been the core of Naga think tank. Angami Phizo was a relative by late entrant (June, 1946). He was "deeply convinced by the Muslim two-nation theory and the tactics employed by the Muslims League to create Pakistan." A failure in all the pursuits in his personal life 'Phizo joined the NNC when it was in the thick of its movement and immediately "tried to prevail upon the organisation to lean more towards extremism." Phizo had a firm belief that if India could concede to the Muslim League, his own pressure tactics would win independence for the Nagas too. Phizo remained an ordinary member of NNC until 1950. It was only in the aftermath of NNC-Akbari Hydari Agreement that Phizo with his rhetoric was able to factionalise the NNC into moderate and extremist sections. Aliba and Sakhrie were realists and pragmatists and hence were dubbed as moderates. The rise of 'extremists' saw the obvious relegation of the moderates into insignificance. In fact Sakhrie was subsequently murdered. The suspicion was again on Phizo.
55. T. Aliba Imti, op. cit., p. 70.
56. Ibid., p. 71.
57. Ibid.
58. Ibid., p. 70.
59. *Ibid.*
60. R.J. Moore, *Endgames of Empire: Studies in Britain's Indian Problem*, Delhi, 1988, p. 75.
61. B. Hansaria, *Sixth Schedule to the Constitution of India: A Study*, Gauhati, 1983, p. 8.
62. Ibid.
63. R.J. Moore, op. cit.

64. Report of the North East Frontier (Assam) Tribal and Excluded Areas Sub-committee (Report) reproduced in B. Hangaria, *Sixth Schedule to the Constitution of India: A Study* (Gauhati, 1983), p. A–183–184.
65. B. Hansaria, op. cit., p. 8.
66. Report, pp. 184–185
67. Report, p. A–184.
68. Ibid.
69. Report, p. A–192.
70. Report, p. A–192.
71. Report, p. A–190.
72. Ibid., p. A–192.
73. Ibid.
74. Report, p. A–194–196.
75. S.K. Chaube, *Hill Politics in North East India*, New Delhi, 1973, p. 162.
76. R.N. Prasad, *Government and Politics in Mizoram*, New Delhi, 1987, p. 80.
77. Report of the North East Frontier Tribal and Excluded Areas Sub-Committee, Vol. II, also with ibid.
78. Ibid.
79. Ibid.
80. Ibid.
81. Ibid.
82. Memorandum to the Bordoloi Committee by Mizo Union, 22-4-1947.
83. Pachunga, Dahrawka and Hmartawnpunga, *Independence*, Aizawl, June 7, 1947.
84. D. Ronghaka, *Zoram Independent*, May 5, 1947.
85. R. Vanlawma, *Khawi Lamah Nge I Kal Dawn? Quo Vadis*, June 18, 1947.
86. R. Sena Samuelson, *Love Mizoram*, Imphal, 1985, p. 51.
87. K. Zawla, *Zoram Din Hmun Dik Hmuh Chuah Theina Tur*, *Aizawl*, July 29, 1947.
88. Ibid.
89. R. Sena Samuelson, op. cit., pp. 47–50.
90. B.B. Goswami, op. *cit.*, 136, S.K. Chaube, op. cit., p. 162, R.N. Prasad, op. cit., p. 255.
91. B. B. Goswami, ibid.
92. This was clarified by Vanlawma, *Ka Ram le Kei*, *Aizawl*, 1972, p. 216.
93. *Mizo Zalenna Pawl: Pawl Din Dan* (United Mizo Freedom Organisation : Constitution), Aizawl, 1947.
94. R.N. Prasad, op. cit., B.B. Goswami, op. cit.
95. Vanlawma, op. cit., p. 217.
96. B.B. Goswami, op. cit.
97. R. Sena Samuelson, op. cit., pp. 47–50.
98. Ibid.
99. *Proceedings of the Accredated Leaders of all Lushai Political Parties*, *Aizawl*, August 14, 1947.

100. *Bhagvati Patrika* (Editorial), 18th August 1947, cited in K.M. Singh, *Hijam Irabot Singh and Political Movements in Manipur*, (Delhi, 1989), p. 251.
101. Bimal Deb and Dilip J. Lahiri, *Manipur: Culture and Politics*, (Delhi, 1987), p. 124, 159.
Niharendu Dutt Majumdar, Minister, Government of West Bengal, wrote to Sardar Patel, Deputy Prime Minister on 14 January 1948 "with regard to the future of the state of Manipur, it is also to be considered whether it should not be merged in West Bengal. . . I think the interests of Manipur will be better served by her merger in West Bengal than in Assam: cited in Kshetri Rajendra Singh, "Social Movements in Manipur: A Study of Two Movements among the Meitheis," unpublished Ph.D. thesis, Centre for Social Studies, Surat, 1987, p. 106. Also in Durga Das (ed.), Sardar Patel's Correspondence, (Ahmedabad, 1973), Vol. 9, p. 253.
102. It had originated in the Manipur State Congress unit and supported by Manipur Socialist Party. It reportedly had Sardar Patel's blessings.
103. Kshetri Rajendra Singh, op. cit.
104. N.Joykumar Singh, "Movement for Responsible Government in Manipur (1938-48)", *Proceedings of the North East India History Association, Barapani Session*, 1983, pp.202–209. Also Khs. Shyam Kanai Singh The Merger of Manipur with India: Proceedings of the NEIHA", Imphal Session, 1982, pp. 224–28.
105. Ibid.
106. Ibid.
107. Ibid.
108. Ibid.
109. Bimal J. Dev and Dilip Lahiri, op. cit.
110. Ibid.
111. Kshetri Rajendra Singh, op. cit., p. 107.
112. Irawat was already talking in terms of a people's republic in Manipur and was working towards it which had reinforced the Indian Governments suspicion. The country was already witnessing peasants unrest in Telangana, Tebhaga (Bengal), Assam and Tripura. The second Congress of the CPI was held in Calcutta during 28th February to 6 March 1948 which supported these movements. This was followed by the inauguration of state unit of CPI at the District Organising Committee level in Manipur. This was a red signal for the Government.
113. S. Chattradhari *Manipungi Itihassta Irawat* (Imphal, 1972), pp. 64–65, cited in Kshetri Rajendra Singh, op. cit., p. 109.
114. See note 99, Also T. Bir Singh, *Comrade Irabot*, (Imphal, 1983), p. 56–57.
115. Kshetri Rajendra Singh, op. cit., p. 111.
116. The Communist armed movement in Manipur had intensified and was viewed seriously by the Government of India specially because it came in the wake of rumour of Chinese hand in it and the spurts of such movements in many parts of the country. Sardar Patel as the Home Minister confirmed in the Parliament (February, 1951)

that there had been a Communist Uprising in Manipur of a serious nature but was presently under control. The Times of India (28 Feb. 1951) wrote in its editorial "widespread terrorist activities are reported in the strategic north-eastern districts embracing Assam, Manipur and Tripura. Peking may not harbour expen sionist designs but communism is potentially expansive and explosive and anxiety is heightened by the Union Home Ministers reference of encouragement for the Assam terrorists from across the border." The communist phobia gripped the Assam Chief Minister Bordoloi so much that he asked Patel to allow Manipur autonomy so that Manipur did not influence Assam.

117. N. Joykumar Singh, op. cit.
118. Ksh. Shyam Kanai Singh, op. cit.
119. N. Joykumar Singh, op. cit.
120. Ibid.
121. Ibid.
122. Ibid.
123. Confidential Report, 27 July 1949, Memo No. 78, CID, from S. Palit, S.P. Manipur to the Dewan.
124. D.O. No. DM.89/49, dated Imphal 29 August, 1949 from Major Rawal Amar Singh to Adviser to the Governor of Assam cited in K.M.M. Singh, op. cit., p. 346.
125. N.J. Joykumar Singh, op. cit.
126. Ibid.
127. Ibid.
128. Proceedings of a public meeting held at Gandhi Maidan, 3rd August, 1949, cited in K.M.M. Singh, op. cit., p. 347.
129. *Prajatantra*, 17 August 1949 in a report by S. Palit, S.P. Manipur to Dewan, 29 August, 1949, in ibid.
130. Resolution of the meeting of MLA's belonging to the ruling Praja Shanti Sabha on 25th August cited in ibid.
131. Ksh. Shyam Kanai Singh, op. cit.
132. op. cit.
133. From the Offg. pvt. Secretary to His Highness, Maharaja of Manipur, 18 September 1949, cited in K.M.M. Singh, op. cit., p. 354.
134. N. Joykumar Singh, op. cit.
135. Maharaja Budhachandra to Shri Prakasa 18-9-1949, reproduced in Resistence, 25 September, 1979.
136. From the Maharaja of Manipur to Sri Prakasa, 18 September 1949, cited in K.M.M. singh, op. cit., p. 354.
137. K.M.M. Singh, op. cit., p. 355.
138. Durga Das, (ed.) op. cit. Vol. 8, p. 528.
139. Nari Rustomji, *The Enchanted Frontier* (Oxford, 1973), p.109, R. Constantine, *Maid of the Mountain* (New Delhi, 1981), pp. 93–94.
140. Sri Prakasa to the Maharaja of Manipur in 19 September 1949, cited in K.M.M. Singh, p. 355.
141. Maharaja Bodh Chandra to Sri Prakasa, 20 September 1949, cited in ibid., p. 357.
142. Shri Prakasa to the Maharaja, 19-9-49, reproduced in The Resistance, 2 October, 1979.

143. *Bhagyavati Patrika* (Editorial), dated 20th September, 1949, courtesy *Resistance*, Vol. IV, No. 40, dated 9th October, 1979, cited in K.M.M. Singh, op. cit., p. 358.
144. *Bhagavati Patrika*, dated 21st September, 1949, courtesy, Resistance, Vol. IV, No. 41, dated 16th October, 1979, cited in ibid.

CONCLUSION

The advent of independence in August 1947, did not signify the end of the long-drawn struggle of the Indians against the British. The immediate task was to strive to avert a possible balkanisation of the country by integrating the areas which showed secessionist tendencies. But it was rendered difficult because of the 'weak-links' of these areas with the mainland. Moreover the political climate of the subcontinent was vitiated by the forces of communalism and separatism. In fact the eve of British withdrawal from India was characterised by two co-eval trends: a pan-Indian sentiment seeking the merger of their areas with the mainland; the other a separatist tendency seeking an independent existence outside India. North East India was no exception to this. But the grounds were different in the region. In the hills of Nagaland or Mizoram or the plains of Manipur the prevalence of such tendencies were not due to political reasons or despotic ambitions but more on cultural and metaphysical considerations. Alt ough the Meithies and the Nagas lived in their present habitat from the proto-historic period, the Mizos migrated only a couple of centuries back. Except the Meitheis, the others escaped the influence of Sanskritisation. Even the Meitheis came under its impact only in the eighteenth century. Thus even if there was interaction between the Indian civilization on the one hand and these communities on the other, the latter could preserve their exclusivity to a great extent.

The British opened the exclusivity of these communities and exposed them to the outer world. There was a combined effort by the colonial administration as well as the Christian missionaries to 'change' the Nagas and the Mizos. (They could not do so with the Meitheis as the nature of political intervention was different.) A modern administration was set up to govern them. A new religion introduced. Modern education and social reform followed. Application of modern elementary science and technology was fostered. These changes detribalised the people to a considerable extent and within a short span of time they were a changed people with a new life, new culture, new morality, religion, a modern identity and more important, a consciousness about this identity. Often this identity created metaphysical confusions for the Nagas and the Mizos. The colonial functionaries constantly fed them with the idea that they were not Indians neither in physical appearance nor in socio-cultural terms but at the same time ruled them as part of British India. So long these tribals identified themselves by their Sub-tribal affiliations but now they were given a generic identity. The advent of British rule also resulted in a metamorphosis of the tribal-non-tribal relationship. The non-tribal living in the border areas were subjected to frequent raids, kidnapping and headhunting from the tribals. The tribal Chiefs considered these areas as their sphere of influence and the people as their subordinate. During the British rule they saw the same plainsmen as the 'babus' in the colonial administration who invariably frowned the 'loose' way of life of the tribals, often ridiculed their morality and dress codes. Hence, the tribals identified 'Indians' synonymously with these 'babus.'

Manipur was a princely state. Hence colonial-intervention in its internal affairs was restricted. But the Indian business community had an unrestricted entry into it who soon monopolised the core sectors and introduced the practice of hoarding and black marketeering. During the inter-war period they often created artificial food crisis and near-famine conditions. Socially too, even though the Meitheis had embraced Hinduism and absorbed the

Brahmanicial order they were not granted equal status as a Hindu and Indian main- land. The result was resentment towards the Indians in general and the exploitative and discriminatory system that it represented in particular. Such was the state of consciousness in the region when the issue of 'merger' emerged. When the British declared their intention to quit India Manipur was reeling under one crisis after another under a feudal order and the oppresiveness of the monarchical system. The people led a State Peoples Movement to successfully install a Assembly of People's representatives and reduce the Maharaja to a nominal Head. There was a rejuvenation of political process with the prospect of Manipur reverting to its pre-British status after the lapse of British paramountcy. The suggestion of Mountbatten to the Princely States to join either of the Dominions (India or Pakistan) and the emergence of such a trend in other Princely States raised a dilemma in Manipur: to join India or remain independent. Given its identification with Hinduism and the following Sanskritisation process, Manipur was already inclined to merge with India. The newly emerged middle class as part of the all-India middle class had a pan-Indian outlook. Hence their political organisation Nikhil Manipuri Mahasabha did not lose time to join the Indian National Congress to expedite the merger. At the same time another trend of apprehension about the prospective life in India was also prevalent. But the post-colonial Indian State preferred to ignore the apprehension as well as the inclination of the Meithies and decided to effect the 'integration' of Manipur in a secretive manner. Despite the existence of Peoples' Assembly, it invited the Maharaja to Shillong, the capital of Assam and used 'bait' and 'pressure tactics' to make him sign the Instrument of Accession. In the process it completely ignored the people and hurt their pride thereby alienating even those majority who were inclined to merge with India.

For the Nagas and Mizos who were complacent under the British rule which they considered paternalistic, there was a similar crisis with the abrupt British declaration to withdraw. Apart from merger and independence, they toyed with another idea: to join Burma with which they were close in race and ethnicity. Their immediate reaction to the British declaration was to form political platforms from which they could represent their case to the outgoing British as well as the Indian leadership. The Nagas formed the Naga National Council while the Mizos formed the Mizo Union. The Nagas submitted successive memoranda to express their fear that they were different from the Indians in every way — from look to outlook; their number were small and they stand the treat to be overwhelmed by the vast majority of Indians. They feared that their land and in the way of life which was so dear to them would be snatched away. But the British chose to ignore their representation and except for one letter from Nehru assuring of protection, the Indian leadership was silent.

The Mizo leader Vanlawma was invited by the Assam Premier Bordoloi for a deal. Bordoloi offered full-fledged membership to the Mizo leader in the Bordoloi Sub-committee which would decide the protective devices for the tribals in the Indian Constitution. In return the Mizo leader agreed to merge with India. But in the mean time on the issue of perpetuation of Chieftainship in Mizoram, the Mizos were polarised into two hostile groups. Since merger with India promised to abolish the oppressive chiefly rule, the majority of the Mizos favoured integration. The representative of this majority officially integrated with India through participation in the Bordoloi Sub-committee which was part of the Constituent Assembly. But the opposing group considered it a breach of agreement by Bordoloi who promised full membership to the Mizos in the committee but now offered only co-opted membership. They propagated this breach as an indication of things to come and opposed the merger. It is this group which subsequently supported a secessionist movement in Mizoram in the 1960s. In the Naga hills Assam Governor Akbar Hydari managed to bring the Naga leaders to the negotiating table and effected a Nine Point agreement by which the Nagas agreed to merge with India. But on the interpretation of the Ninth Clause, disagreement emerged again. The Naga leaders insisted that this integration was for a period of ten year only following which they would be free to opt out of India. The Government felt that the Clause provided only for a change in the arrangement. Thus while on the basis of this agreement the Naga hills were integrated with the Indian Union, the Nagas continued to view this agreement as void due to mutual disagreement over its interpretation.

As can be seen the seeds of disintegration were inherent in the agreement of integration. The Meitheis had apprehension about the Indians, the Nagas fear while the Mizos had hope from the integration. The belying of this hope or the actualisation of the fear or apprehension could tilt the balance against such integration. Since then, therefore, the integration of these areas had always been fragile and the Indian State always on the edge.

BIBLIOGRAPHY

Abbi, B.I. *North Eastern Region — Problem and Perspectives*, Chandigarh, 1985.

Chaube, S.K. *Hill Politics in North Eastern India*, New Delhi, 1973.

Constantine, B.K. *Manipur: Maid of the Mountains*, New Delhi, 1980.

Dev, B.J. and Lahiri D. *Manipur: Culture and Politics*, Delhi, 1987.

Elwin, Verrier *Nagaland*, Shillong, 1961.

Goswami, B.B. *Mizo Unrest: A Study of Politicisation of Culture*, Jaipur, 1979.

Horam, M. *Thirty Years of Naga Insurgency*, New Delhi, 1990.

Imti, T. Aliba *Reminiscences: From Impur to Naga National Council*, Mokokchong, 1988.

Kabui, G. and others *History of Manipur*, Imphal, 1991.

Nibedon, N. *Mizoram: Daggers Brigade*, New Delhi, 1980. *Nagaland: Night of the Guerillas*, New Delhi, 1989. *North East; Ethnic Explosion*, New Delhi, 1989.

North East India History Association Proceedings. Select volumes.

Phadnis, U. *Ethnicity and National Building in South Asia*, New Delhi, 1991.

Rustomji, N. *Enchanted Frontiers*, New Delhi, 1971. *Imperilled Frontiers*, New Delhi, 1989.

Sarkar, S. *Modern India*, New Delhi, 1982.

Samuelson, R.S. *Love Mizoram*, Imphal, 1985.

Sareen, H. *Insurgency in North East India*, New Delhi, 1982. *North East in Flames, New Delhi*, 1986.

Singh, K.M. *Hijam Irabot and Political Movements in Manipur*, New Delhi, 1979.

Singh, Joykumar *Social Movements in Manipur*, New Delhi, 1992.

Venkata Rao, V. *Century of Government and Politics in North East India*; Vols on Nagaland, Manipur and Mizoram, New Delhi, 1987-1991.

Vanlawma, *Ka Ram le kei*, (in Mizo), Aizawl, 1972.

Vumson, *Zo History*, Aizawl n.d.

Yonou, Assoso, *The Rising Nagas: A Political and Historical Study*, Delhi, 1974.

R. J. BARENDSE received his B.A. in Modern History from the University of Amsterdam, and his M.A. in the History of European Expansion and his Ph.D in History from Leiden University. Associate Research Fellow at the International Institute for Asian Studies/Faculty of Social Science, Amsterdam, Dr. Barendse has been a visiting scholar at the Indian Council of Historical Research; a senior researcher at the Faculty of History, Erasmus University, Rotterdam; a research fellow at the International Institute for Asian Studies, Leiden; and a visiting scholar at the Australian National University.

Dr. Barendse has published, in addition to many articles and reviews, *The Arabian Seas 1640-1700* (CNWS, Leiden, 1998 — an earlier version of this work), with O. Nieuwenhuys, *Kinderen in India hun leven en werk* (Children in India: Their Life and Work — Utrecht, 1987), and *Een geschiedenis van Engeland in de twintigste eeuw van 1900 tot 1990* (English History in the Twentieth Century — uitgeverij het Balans, Amsterdam, 2001).

